composition STUDIES

Vol

Editor
Jennifer Clary-Lemon

Book Review Editor
Asao B. Inoue

Editorial Assistant
Kirstian Lezubski
Graeme Coleman

Former Editors
Gary Tate
Robert Mayberry
Christina Murphy
Peter Vandenberg
Ann George
Carrie Leverenz
Brad E. Lucas

Advisory Board

Linda Adler-Kassner
*University of California,
Santa Barbara*

Tom Amorose
Seattle Pacific University

Chris Anson
North Carolina State University

Valerie Balester
Texas A&M University

Robert Brooke
University of Nebraska, Lincoln

Sidney Dobrin
University of Florida

Lisa Ede
Oregon State University

Paul Heilker
*Virginia Polytechnic Institute
and State University*

James Inman
*University of Maryland
University College*

Laura Micciche
University of Cincinnati

Peggy O'Neill
Loyola College

Victor Villanueva
Auburn University

SUBSCRIPTIONS
Composition Studies is published twice each year (May and November). Subscription rates: Individuals $25 (Domestic) and $30 (International); Institutions $75 (Domestic) and $75 (International); Students $15.

BACK ISSUES
Recent back issues are now available through Amazon.com for $12. To find issues, use the advanced search feature and search on "Composition Studies" (title) and "Parlor Press" (publisher). Photocopies of earlier issues are available for $3.

BOOK REVIEWS
Assignments are made from a file of potential book reviewers. To have your name added to the file, send a current vita to the Book Review Editor at asao@inoueweb.com.

SUBMISSIONS
All appropriate essay submissions will be blind reviewed by two external readers. Manuscripts should be 3,500-7,500 words and conform to current MLA guidelines for format and documentation; they should be free of author's names and other identifying references. *Electronic submissions are preferred*: consult our Web site for details. (For print submissions, submit three titled, letter-quality copies with a cover letter including the title and author contact information, loose postage sufficient to mail manuscripts to two reviewers, and a #10 SASE for the return of reviewer comments.) *Composition Studies* will not consider previously published manuscripts. We discourage the submission of conference papers that have not been revised or extended for a critical reading audience. Those wishing to submit Course Designs should first consult our Web site for specific instructions. Letters to the editor and responses to articles are strongly encouraged.

To ensure a blind review, *Composition Studies* requests
1. The authors of the document have deleted their names from the text, with "Author" and year used in the references and endnotes, instead of the authors' name, article title, etc.
2. With Microsoft Office documents, author identification should also be removed from the properties for the file (see under File in Word), by clicking on the following, beginning with File on the main menu of the Microsoft application: File > Save As > Tools (or Options with a Mac) > Security > Remove personal information from file properties on save > Save.
3. With PDFs, the authors' names should also be removed from Document Properties found under File on Adobe Acrobat's main menu.

Direct all correspondence to:

>Jennifer Clary-Lemon, Editor
>Department of Rhetoric, Writing, and Communications
>University of Winnipeg
>515 Portage Avenue, Winnipeg, MB R3B 2E9
>Canada

Composition Studies *is grateful for the generous support of the Dean of Arts and the Department of Rhetoric, Writing, and Communications at the University of Winnipeg.*

© Copyright 2011 by Jennifer Clary-Lemon, Editor
Production and printing is managed by Parlor Press, www.parlorpress.com.
ISSN 1534-9322

www.compositionstudies.uwinnipeg.ca

composition STUDIES

Volume 40, Number 1
Spring 2012

articles

Forgotten Radicals: A History of the Term "Theory" in Three Decades of WPA Scholarship   **9**
Brian Ray

"So what are *we* working on?" Pronouns as a Way of Re-Examining Composing   **24**
Kate Pantelides and Mariaelena Bartesaghi

Undergraduate Writing Majors and the Rhetoric of Professionalism   **39**
Christian Weisser and Laurie Grobman

An Emerging Model for Student Feedback: Electronic Distributed Evaluation   **60**
Beth Brunk-Chavez and Annette Arrigucci

What's in a Coauthor?: (Re)Locating Joseph Denney in Composition History   **78**
Ivan Davis

course design

Teaching as Text—The Pedagogy Seminar: LIT 730, Teaching Composition   **95**
Janet Auten

book reviews

Narrative Inquiry: Approaches to Language and Literacy Research, by David Schaafsma and Ruth Vinz   **113**
Jaqueline McLeod Rogers

Everyday Genres: Writing Assignments across the Disciplines, by Mary Soliday   **116**
Irene L. Clark

The Changing of Knowledge in Composition: Contemporary Perspectives, edited by Lance Massey and Richard C. Gebhardt   **120**
    Adam M. Pacton

Going North Thinking West, by Irvin Peckham   **124**
    Chanon Adsanatham

Gramsci and Educational Thought, edited by Peter Mayo   **128**
    Kristin Mock

Writing Against the Curriculum: Anti-Disciplinarity in the Writing and Cultural Studies Classroom, edited by Randi Gray Kristensen and Ryan M. Claycomb   **132**
    Kenny Walker

Cross-Language Relations in Composition, edited by Bruce Horner, Min-Zhan Lu, and Paul Kei Matsuda   **135**
    Amanda Athon

Digital Griots: African American Rhetoric in a Multimedia Age, by Adam J. Banks   **139**
    Jeanne Law Bohannon

The Managerial Unconscious in the History of Composition Studies, by Donna Strickland   **143**
    Kristine Johnson

Beyond Postprocess, edited by Sidney I. Dobrin, Jeff A. Rice, and Michael Vastola   **147**
    Timothy Oleksiak

Rhetoric's Earthly Realm: Heidegger, Sophistry, and the Gorgian Kairos, by Bernard Alan Miller   **151**
    Ira Allen

contributors   155

Forgotten Radicals: A History of the Term "Theory" in Three Decades of WPA Scholarship

Brian Ray

> This article contests the prevailing assumption that composition scholarship has only recently begun to theorize the role of the writing program administrator. While many contemporary scholars accept the idea that the field mainly offered practical "how-to" articles early on in its history, the author rereads work from past decades to show otherwise. The recovery of these articles offers valuable insights into current debates about the place of theory in WPA work by strengthening the view that theory is a vital and inseparable element of intellectual inquiry. This article also strives to enable a more dynamic understanding of the ways that WPAs harness theory to articulate and accomplish their agendas.

WPA scholarship has directly engaged the theory-practice binary in recent years to empower administrators and promote their value in the academy. Notable contributions to this endeavor include Shirley K. Rose and Irwin Weiser's *The Writing Program Administrator as Theorist*, Donna Strickland and Jeanne Gunner's *The Writing Program Interrupted*, Susan H. McLeod's *Writing Program Administration*, Linda Adler-Kassner's *The Activist WPA*, and a number of articles that have appeared in composition studies journals in the years following CWPA's 1998 position statement "Evaluating the Intellectual Work of Writing Administration." These works present theory as a way to "not only question the power, methods, and institutional function" that regulate the position, but also as an avenue "toward the disruption of those very powers, methods, and roles" in order to earn WPAs greater agency (Dobrin 70). However, they presume that prior to the last few years, particularly during the 1980s and 1990s, WPAs struggled to articulate the nature of their scholarship while emphasizing conservative issues such as professionalization and institutional identity. I offer an alternative reading of scholarship from the past three decades to show that, from its inception, WPA discourse has theorized the administrative position while also embracing less conservative, more subversive ideologies. Recognizing this earlier discourse of theoretical self-reflection should provide an even greater rationale for the use of theory in WPA work by positioning it as internal and natural rather than alien and artificial. A realization of the theory-practice binary as a fiction also enables a more dynamic understanding of theory and its potential to help create and debate new directions for writing programs.

As John Trimbur notes, the professionalization of WPAs has recently led to "a troubled conscience, signified by the figure of the 'boss compositionist' and feelings of complicity in an exploitative labor system," feelings that scholars in the recent volume *The Writing Program Interrupted* address candidly ("Introduction" ix). In the first article in this collection, Jeff Rice challenges what he sees as the conservative and anti-theoretical attitudes of WPAs who generally "reject [theory] out of hand as 'impractical,' opting to maintain conservative positions regarding their work in very public ways" (2). Rice finds the alleged absence of theorists such as Stuart Hall, Jacques Derrida, and Michel Foucault from WPA discourse "suspicious" (6), and he goes on to ask "Without these or similar theories, can we think about programmatic moves without falling back on the familiar? How can we think about programmatic decisions in terms of those theoretical positions that have done much work to challenge status quo positions ... Or can we?" (6).

Rice's critique does effectively encourage WPAs to scrutinize the assumptions that underlie "the language, texts, and position statements that have given them strength as professionals and a feeling of academic legitimacy," in order to "move away from the conservative tropes and values that have come to dominate our work" (12). These tropes include general appeals to stability, consistency, and pedagogical soundness, and can be seen in documents, such as the 2000 WPA Outcomes Statement, that speak to a broad audience by circumventing any need "for agreement on a single best way to achieve those outcomes" (White qtd. in Rice 11). At the same time, Rice and other scholars in *The Writing Program Interrupted* have constructed their own reductive narratives, essentializing theory as a concept that only disrupts and interrogates conservative foundations while offering the barest sketch of an alternative. For example, Dobrin challenges WPAs via Nietzsche, Deleuze, and Foucault to "create possibilities through disruption, or, at minimum, Foucault's notion of thinking 'differently'" (70). The liberal narrative possesses its own attractive tropes of disruption and anti-conformity that do not necessarily inspire the change it envisions. Just as we all tend to value consistency, we also tend to value thinking differently—regardless of how theoretical we might interpret our actions and situations. The liberal discourse merely creates a narrative of Us (free-thinking theorists) versus Them (anti-theoretical conservatives) that clouds, rather than clarifies, how theory informs writing program administration.

My reading of WPA scholarship from the past thirty years, however, reveals a much wider diversity of theorizing than the current narratives acknowledge, and therefore offers a more nuanced approach that builds on Rose and Weiser's inclusive definition of theory as "a general explanation of some phenomena" ("Theorizing" 186) that "do[es] not tell us what to do" but rather tells us "how to understand" and how "to think about how to act" (191). Their definition, drawing on Phelps' view of theory and practice as "recursive and reciprocal" (qtd. in "Theorizing" 188), serves as a productive starting point. After giving an account of the conventional view of WPA scholarship, I will map an alternative history of how theory has manifested in four distinct modes since 1979. These modes form a continuum of theoretical action rather than a series of dichotomies between practical and theoretical work. First, theory manifests as the analysis of an issue through an existing theoretical lens. For example, Dobrin uses Nietzsche, Deleuze, and Foucault to challenge conservative WPA narratives. Second, theory can manifest as the production of an original explanation or account of writing or writing program administration. Raúl Sánchez has advocated for more production of such original theories in the field of composition. Third, theory can manifest as the implementation of theoretical ideas through policies, curricula, and WPAs' day-to-day decisions. Last, theory can manifest in acts (including scholarship) that blend the previous three modes of theorizing.

By exploring the early theoretical discourse, my article answers Jeanne Gunner's call for scholarship that goes beyond the "conflict-free, apolitical activities" that an existing hegemonic discourse has already deemed appropriate for administrative work—namely professionalization and disciplinary identity (274). I see a crucial importance in following Gunner's caution for WPA scholars to "remain mindful of cultural critiques of the position and its social functions" (264). However, this article also performs the critique of grand narratives that Dobrin encourages, not simply by overturning conservative values but by also resisting the counter-narrative that liberal WPAs have established. By interpreting this overlooked scholarship against polarizing narratives, I offer a third-way, a liminal space, of discussing WPA theory that moves between and across boundaries.

Remapping the Conservative Narrative of the 1980s

A distinct assumption in the field exists that WPAs have only recently turned from professionalization and praxis to theory as a resource for their work. Although CWPA was founded in 1976 at an energetic MLA Convention session, a national discourse crystallized in 1978 when the council began to publish *WPA*, an outgrowth of its newsletter. Susan McLeod discusses the struggle for professionalization during the 1980s, a time when "the position ... became a revolving door at many institutions" (74) because administration was considered service rather than scholarship. McLeod emphasizes professionalization as the primary concern of this decade as well as the 1990s, citing the work of Christine Hult as invaluable in the drafting of "The Portland Resolution" in 1992 and "Evaluating the Intellectual Work of Writing Program Administrators" in 1998. Both documents, McLeod writes, "have helped raise the professional status of the WPA" (77). As she looks to the future, McLeod also compares the broader, more theoretical questions of WPAs today with the "very practical, hands-on issues" in "the early issues of *CCC* and *WPA*" published thirty years ago (78). Her conclusion is that within the last ten years WPAs have developed much more sophisticated, theory-based foundations that legitimize their work. My reading of WPA scholarship suggests otherwise—that the 1980s did witness theoretical as well as practical engagements of writing program administration. These theoretical positions have simply gone unacknowledged by both conservative and liberal WPA discourses that have accepted existing accounts of the position's evolution.

In particular, these dominant discourses rely on a few retrospectives and other essays appearing during the 1980s that offered meta-commentary on WPA scholarship. One such retrospective was published by Kenneth Bruffee in 1985, claiming that WPA scholarship had evolved largely due to an increasing sense of identity and professionalization (see "The WPA"). A later retrospective by Christine Hult, "The Scholarship of Administration" asserts a similar paradigm, with an added observation that WPAs had begun to rethink the nature of their work as an intellectual endeavor. Considering trends in *WPA*'s volumes prior to 1985, Bruffee first observes that "the topics that concern WPAs have not changed very much in the past decade," whereas the "sophistication and knowledgeability with which we are addressing [them]" had indeed ("The WPA" 5). He locates this increase in sophistication not within the development of theories for WPA work but instead within a shift from "how-to" articles to ones concerned with "professional identity" (7), and he praises the development as indicative of progress. The five articles Bruffee describes as addressing professional identity are of special interest to him because each one "helps us tell ourselves who we are" through self discovery and self-critique (7). But Bruffee's idea of self-critique mainly involves the absence of "white wash" in describing a "program's failures as well as its successes," and responding intelligently to criticism—as he notes in the retrospective when discussing a review of Witte and Faigley's *Evaluating College Writing Programs* (9). There is no indication that such self-critique goes beyond this sense of objectivity.

A rereading of the *WPA* archives between 1978 and 1985 reveals a handful of articles that explicitly engage theories not only of writing but also, as Elaine Maimon states, "its place in the curriculum" (11). My reading of *WPA*'s archives prior to 1985 show at least four articles that conceive of theory as a vital component to a WPA's goals and responsibilities. These articles share a common concern with the need for consistent program philosophies, grounded in theory, to design coherent course sequences while articulating their value to the larger university. For these authors, theory becomes a means of reflection and action, and also of enhancing the WPA's agency. Each of these articles theorizes according to Rose and Weiser's definition: either by analyzing problems through a theoretical lens, presenting an original theory to account for WPA work, describing ways to implement theories through program design, or a combination thereof.

The first of these articles, Greg Larkin's 1979 "The Essential Unity of Language Arts Programs," presents a theory of writing and its role in the university in order to assist WPAs in constructing a coherent course sequence. Larkin does not cite theorists by name, as Rice would require, but rather offers an original explanation of writing program administration to address a set of problems. Rather than discuss professional identity, Larkin theorizes solutions to what he calls "conceptual fragmentation," which he defines as the lack of a guiding philosophy for the construction of writing courses (25). To untangle the "contradictory premises, methods, and materials" of a fragmented program, Larkin proposes "theoretical and practical" steps for bringing "units into a larger whole" (25). For Larkin, "The theoretical ground of all the courses which we as language program administrators supervise is that all lasting language products are the result of conscious, consistent, and purposeful choices by their creators" (26). He goes on to suggest that, "If we accept this basic theory underpinning all the language arts, we can refer to it as we define the specific language skills sought in our various courses" (27). Larkin's theory identifies three major components of writing: thesis and support, expectations and fulfillment, and the idea of order. These three theoretical concepts provide a foundation for coherent program structure, as opposed to a seemingly random sequence that students complete merely to fulfill degree requirements. Consequently, this theory for curriculum design provides a guide to action for WPAs, which is intended to raise the value of composition courses among students and, by extension, university officials.

Although Larkin's framework seems to promote some of the commonplaces about order and consistency that Rice critiques, he nonetheless clearly enunciates a theory to support his agenda. Advocates of poststructural theory will likely disagree with conceptions of writing founded on the fulfillment of expectation, given that postmodernism relies on a conceivably infinite deferral or frustration of that fulfillment. But this does not render Larkin's position anti-theoretical or strictly practical. Here we merely see conflicting theories about the function of language.

The theoretical attention to how writing programs function within the university also serves as a precursor to WAC movements that began taking shape in the mid-1980s. Thomas Dunn's 1980 article "Writing in the Sciences" theorizes similarities between writing in the humanities and the sciences, where "the nonverbal nature of much scientific thought" requires writing mainly as a mode of transmission (12). Although this view of writing is no longer tenable in our field, Dunn nonetheless clearly offers a theory to support a claim that science programs need to develop writing courses at the introductory and upper levels. Dunn's theory of writing holds that "literature [as opposed to scientific articles] ... seems to me to serve four functions" that consist of conveying perceptions, analyzing such perceptions, evoking emotions, and finally synthesizing the first three components to "leave the reader with an added dimension of understanding, an overall or gestalt sense of the subject at large" (12). Dunn very clearly offers a theory of writing's purpose, and he uses these four criteria to argue that writing in the sciences aims for the same purpose, albeit through "logic and precision" (13). He goes on to argue that "scientists do seek to evoke excitement and even wonder and awe in their work" in a manner similar to literature in that both forms of writing "transmit experience" (14). Although contemporary

WPAs will likely dismiss Dunn's use of the term "literature" as an umbrella for all non-scientific writing, the article is historically relevant. Like Larkin's piece, it resists any of Bruffee's three categories of how-to, how-to in context, and professional identity.

Also like Larkin, Dunn does not analyze situations through existing theoretical lenses but proposes an original idea that pushes on the boundaries of then-conventional purviews of WPAs—the staffing and oversight of programs whose policies and curricula, as Gary A. Olson and Joseph M. Moxley observed in their 1989 "Directing Freshman Composition: The Limits of Authority," were decided by department chairs. The article theorizes in only one of the four possible manifestations, since Dunn does not offer specifics regarding how to implement such courses. Its relevance to WPAs lies in an orientation to writing from a wider institutional perspective. Dunn encourages administrators to think beyond the first-year writing course as a field of reflection and action.

Elaine Maimon's 1981 article "Writing in the Arts and Sciences" theorizes WPA work in all four of the possible modes by offering a theory of administration that also promotes the execution of existing composition theories. This article also makes the first clear call for administrators to "think differently," as Dobrin paraphrases Foucault (70), in writing program administration's scholarly history. Maimon addresses the importance of theory in regard to the development of writing courses that prepare students for a university's broader curriculum. Advocating an early version of WAC, Maimon asserts that "A consistent theoretical formulation [of a writing program] requires many English teachers to break old mind-sets and to reflect seriously on unexamined prejudices about teaching composition" (9). In Maimon's view, theories of writing are not only relevant to teachers but to WPAs, who must integrate these theories into their work as administrators.

Maimon maintains that the success of a writing program hinges on "a consistent philosophy of writing and its place in the curriculum" (11). She speaks specifically about the design of writing courses that engage a university's entire curriculum and cooperation with faculty across the disciplines to do so. The formation of a consistent philosophical or theoretical base for the purpose of writing is essential to this task. She even encourages administrators to read James Kinneavy's *A Theory of Discourse* "for a theoretical perspective that allows us to value styles beyond the belletristic" (11). Maimon identifies theory as the core element of a WPA's resources. Perhaps most importantly, this theoretical position on WPA work does not draw a binary between the conservative commonplaces of consistency and pedagogical soundness on the one hand and radical critique on the other. As the liberal discourse currently advocates, Maimon envisions a community of WPAs who value diverse writing styles, implement new theories about writing (Kinneavy's theories being new in 1981), and develop their own philosophies about the function of writing instruction in their institutions.

Finally, William Gracie's 1982 article "Directing Freshman English" further blurs the contemporary divide between theory and practice, as well as the divide between conservative and liberal. Gracie defines WPAs as agents of change who "translate theory into practice" (21). But he also recognizes WPAs not only as translators of theory but makers of it. As he says, "It is by *making* this knowledge" of composition's place in the "institution's curriculum as a whole" that "WPAs are most likely to make an impact on their institutions" (24, emphasis mine). He goes on to say that "However pure and theoretical their own research and that of the authors they read ... WPAs have to be engineers. They have to make their own thought, and the thought of others, practical, applicable, efficient, and effective" (24). This articulation of the WPA recognizes both liberal and conservative values while asserting their interdependency. For Gracie, as well as Maimon, successful WPAs are well-versed in pure theory, they possess the capabilities to make their own pure theories, and they also know how to convey and implement those theories as they negotiate institutional constraints. Furthermore, the analogy of WPAs to engineers embraces theory in a way that subsequent analogies in the 1990s to dancers and musicians do not. While a talented musician may not necessarily be informed about the latest theories of music, engineers must by necessity know how to develop and apply theories to their work. And while performers may engage theories of their arts, they do not necessarily themselves theorize. Meanwhile, engineers are likely not only to draw on others' theories but to imagine their own.

Other articles in *WPA* theorize writing program administration through one or more of the four modes while advocating for changes in program design from clearly articulated socio-political positions. They also eschew the typical activities of professional developments such as grand-scale conferences and keynote speakers. For example, John Trimbur's 1983 article "Students or Staff: Thoughts on the Use of Peer Tutors in Writing Centers" reflects on the administrative practices of writing center administrators, asking "what happens when we institutionalize practices that previously emerged spontaneously, outside of the conventional academic structure," adding that the question is especially important for "those of us who administer writing programs and writing centers" (33). The liberatory elements of Trimbur's article are clear, although he uses theory implicitly, as when he critiques the academic hierarchy for exploiting undergraduate writing center tutors, thereby "alienating tutors from their own activity" and "making them part of a division of labor they neither design nor control" (36). Trimbur proposes that WPAs should see their tutors not only as employees but as students and partners. The article does not focus on the "how-to" aspects of organizing or running writing centers, nor on the professional status of administrators, but instead on the political and ideological reasons for, and consequences of, decentering the administrator's power and sharing it with tutors.

In fact, some trends in WPA discourse actively resist some of the conventions of professional development. A 1985 conference report, titled "'Writing and Undergraduate Education,'" also by Trimbur, describes the first meeting of the New England Conference of Writing Program Administrators as a venue where "There were no major speakers, no call for papers, no formal presentations which would cast conference participants in the role of spectators" (59). Instead the conference was devoted exclusively to group discussions and workshops, such as "a fictional case-study of 'Platonic College'" (60). This workshop presented participants with the task of writing a program philosophy and curriculum to guide staffing and training decisions for a hypothetical college. Thus some of the markings of professionalization and status—calls for papers, keynote speakers—were not only neglected, but devalued. That Trimbur would praise the lack of these status markers reveals a set of values that conflicts with the dominant story of WPAs becoming more professional in order to combat their marginalization in the academy. For certain WPA scholars, the path to increased authority and agency did not lay in apolitical activities of professionalization. Instead, academic spaces and cultural forms such as the conference provided opportunities to subvert the status quo.

This conference report also illustrates a unified understanding of the complex relationship between theory and program administration. As Trimbur writes,

> One of the prevailing undercurrents that surfaced periodically ... sometimes quite sharply ... was the tension between theory and practice, between the desire to articulate a theoretical underpinning for what we do and the daily practical need to put a program in place and make it work. (60)

The conference participants situated themselves as both theorists and program administrators. They were aware that they generated theoretical understandings of their programs and their pedagogical missions, and then implemented them. The importance of theory in WPA work, in all of its manifestations, is clear here.

Despite the complex and sophisticated awareness of theory and practice among many scholars in the 1980s, an ambivalence about theory's importance evolved in the late 1980s and 1990s as WPAs struggled to define research and scholarship in a way that legitimized their work. The struggle is not only evident in *WPA* but also in other journals. For example, two important articles appearing in 1989 speak to the unease among WPAs about their status within the academy and the intellectual value of their work. Wendy Bishop and Gay Lynn Crossley's article "Doing the Hokey Pokey? Why Writing Program Administrators' Job Conditions Don't Seem to Be Improving" describes the insurmountable workload of WPAs despite their recognition as specialists by other faculty department chairs. The other article, Gary A. Olson and Joseph M. Moxley's "Directing Freshman Composition," notes that while WPAs were over-tasked they were also paradoxically "administratively constrained" (56). According to their survey, many English department chairs unfortunately still saw WPAs as supervisors, unqualified to engage in activities such as curriculum reform or program development. In other words, WPAs could carry out the policies of department chairs but did not necessarily possess the authority to re-vision their own writing programs. The oncoming decade would see a definite increase in the attention to the perception of WPA work and scholarship, including debates on how to appropriately define such work.

Remapping the Tensions of the 1990s

In the 1990s, a narrative of the WPA as scholar developed that limited the potential of theory. At times, this narrative even appears to go beyond ambivalence about theory into active resistance toward identifying scholarship as such. When describing the value of writing program administration, *WPA*'s second editor, Christine Hult, offered a position on the nature of WPA work at the end of her editorship in 1994—appearing not in *WPA* but a separate collection entitled *Theorizing and Enacting Difference*. Hult sees WPA work as applying theory via the creation of dynamic programs, rather than generating theories of the position or its functions. For Hult, administration is "theory-based" (126). WPAs apply theory, but they do not produce it. In addition to drawing on Ernest Boyer's *Scholarship Reconsidered*, Hult's article echoes an earlier 1987 piece by Richard Bullock, "When Administration Becomes Scholarship," in which WPA scholarship is described in terms of "an architect's erection of a building or a playwright's successful direction of his or her own play" (14). Hult's piece forwards this analogy as she describes the evolution of scholarship from "how-to" and "professional identity" articles to ones characterized by "systematic, theory-based production of a dynamic program" (126), rather than the conventional texts of scholars in other fields.

Neither Hult nor Bullock recognizes the important distinction between "theory-based production" of a writing program and scholarship that theorizes the roles and actions of the WPA alone. Essentially, Hult only sees *WPA* articles engaged in describing the shape and design of living writing programs. Hult's metaphors for WPA scholarship—music, dance, and theatrical productions (126)—seek to define administration through alternative forms of applied intellectual work. This definition overlooks the fact that WPA scholars such as Dunn, Larkin, Maimon, and Gracie had in fact constructed theories of writing program administration itself, rather than simply applying ready-made ones. While these retrospectives situate theory-based administration as a pragmatic and often creative enterprise, similar to playwriting and musical performance, they paradoxically cast WPAing in terms that make it seem expressivist, non-critical, or non-theoretical.

Meanwhile, major voices in WPA discourse discouraged theorizing as a means to enhance legitimacy and agency. Kenneth Bruffee's keynote address at the 1998 WPA Summer Conference in Arizona (published in 1999) represents the most overt resistance to theory in WPA work and scholarship, the type of resistance that might warrant Rice's criticism of conservative ideologies. Here Bruffee states that "To theorize a boundary practice like WPAing is ... more likely to cauterize that practice, codify it, and conceptualize it—in short, bureaucratize it," ("Thoughts" 63) than to strengthen it. The narrow representation of theory given here limits the agency of WPAs by perpetuating an image of the position that can only implement theories of writing in a manner similar to Hult's. Bruffee widens the theory-practice binary by casting theory as a codifying practice rather than a flexible mode of analysis and reflection. The difference between Bruffee's significant use of theory to explore collaborative group work and his denial of theory in 1998 drives a wedge between teaching and administration, labeling them as distinct activities. This statement does not indict Bruffee so much as it illustrates the state of affairs by the end of the decade. Liberals and conservatives in Composition Studies had battled on many fronts ranging from social constructionism and the abolition of composition to language diversity and also (evidently) writing program administration.

But Bruffee's remarks also anticipate a significant shift in the discourse about theory during the late 1990s, as WPA scholars sought greater recognition for their scholarly contributions. To dissuade a large audience from theorizing suggests that attitudes and perceptions had already begun to move in that direction. Although the late 1990s marks a turning point in the recognition of WPA work, it was less a sudden turn to theory than a strengthening interest in what some WPA scholars had been asserting for at least a decade. In addition to the 1998 statement "Evaluating the Intellectual Work of Writing Program Administrators," articles began to appear that defined WPAs as theorists in their own right. Donald Bushman's "The WPA as Pragmatist," for example, defines administration and its scholarship as "a complex, experimental activity" and "an intellectual undertaking that is concerned with action and reflection" (40). Although such articles did not always invoke the word "theory," they no longer made efforts to avoid couching WPA work in theoretical terms. The next decade would bring about the publication of several titles disregarding Bruffee's warning.

The Past Decade

Following the 1998 position statement on the intellectual work of WPAs, more scholarship about WPA work began to appear in other journals. This wave of scholarship signaled a return to the embrace of theory evident in articles from the early and mid-1980s, except that these articles gave little indication that writing program administration had ever been theorized. The field's flagship journal, *CCC*, began to publish a number of articles about writing program administration. Prior to then, *CCC* had published very few. Richard Bullock addresses the trend in his 2000 review of Diana George's edited collection *Kitchen Cooks, Plate Twirlers, and Troubadours* and Rose and Weiser's *The Writing Program Administrator as Researcher*, noting the appearance of "isolated essays in other journals" than *WPA*

(673). Bullock declares that "an outburst of scholarly activity occurred in 1999 with the publication of no fewer than three book-length collections on writing program administration" (673). This outburst has been followed by the regular appearance of articles and reviews concerning WPA work, including at least a dozen in *CCC* alone. Additionally, *Composition Studies* has published at least three articles on WPA work in addition to ten reviews of books such as Adler-Kassner's *The Activist WPA* and Barbara L'Eplattenier and Lisa Mastrangelo's *Historical Studies of Writing Program Administration*. Other journals that have published articles on WPA work for the first time in the last few years include *Rhetoric Review* and *JAC*.

Over the last ten years, then, WPAs have theorized their positions with increasing frequency across the field's major publications. Although analysis of administrative issues through literary and cultural theory does not overwhelm the field, there is not exactly a vacuum that would indicate a conservative agenda to silence or exclude dissent. Rather, the past decade reflects not only a resurgent interest in WPA scholarship but also a wider healing of the tensions between theory and practice that characterized the 1990s. This trend is evident early on, as in Lauren Sewell Coulter's 2000 *WPA* article "Lean Mean Grading Machines," which provides an excellent case in point with its subtitle "A Bourdieuian Reading of Novice Instructors in a Portfolio-Based Writing Program." Coulter applies Pierre Bourdieu's concept of symbolic violence, "the ability of dominant members of a field to wield their cultural capital as a kind of weapon" (36), to portfolio assessment groups in which experienced instructors' interventions "frustrate efforts to help new graduate instructors feel authoritative about teaching writing" (36). Her theoretical analysis of first-time graduate instructors at her institution challenges the conventional wisdom that scoring groups reduce grade inflation and lead to fairer portfolio evaluation. Rather than confirming Bruffee's fear of theory codifying knowledge, this kind of theorizing enables new perspectives on common administrative practices and speaks back to the discursive authority of existing scholarship.

As another example, Tarez Samra Graban and Kathleen J. Ryan explicitly theorize WPA work in the 2005 *WPA* article "From 'What Is' to 'What Is Possible,'" in which they assert "a particular theoretical understanding of curricular reform and document revision" via *techne*, a term which the authors adapt from Atwill's discussion of Aristotle in *Rhetoric Reclaimed* (90). The authors' definition of WPA work as *techne* recasts curriculum reform as an act that forms "dialogical sites that reflect and construct the programs they represent" and so "become[s] a means for changing that system" (90). For the authors, theorizing does not lead to the formation of inert bodies of knowledge but instead toward the recognition of writing programs as complex, evolving systems that require flexible strategies for knowledge production. The use of Aristotelian terminology might strike some scholars as traditional or conservative, but it might seem revolutionary to others. Either way, it certainly synthesizes existing and original theories in a manner that fulfills the liberal agenda of changing or subverting dominant paradigms. Like many of the essays I have considered, then, Graban and Ryan's work resists easy categorization as conservative or liberal, theoretical or practical.

Even more recently, Debra Frank Dew directly addresses the change in material conditions that result from theorizing WPA work and writing instruction in her article "WPA as Rhetor: Scholarly Production and the Difference a Discipline Makes." Describing the implementation of theories in the execution of daily program activities, Dew goes beyond the conservative narrative of professionalization and emphasizes the use of theory to realize her goals of greater agency and legitimacy at her institution. Although Dew does not apply specific theorists to her situations, she nonetheless frames program administration as a series of rhetorical strategies worthy of intellectual merit. In this sense, her work meets Rose and Weiser's definition of theory while also complicating the narrative of conservative versus liberal WPAs. For example, Dew describes the transformation of "monthly norming" meetings into "curricular review and development sessions" (50). Accordingly, "As the new theoretical work arose faculty rightfully expected institutional support" and over the course of five years salaries gradually increased by thirty percent (50). While this strategy ostensibly plays to the conservative tropes of consistency and professionalization, Dew has also answered the persistent call of *The Writing Program Interrupted* for scholarship that unifies program development with the alleviation of material conditions.

Salary increases did not follow solely from professionalization, but also through Dew's strategic theorizing of her role as a WPA. Another example involves an annual brunch held at the university chancellor's home. Theorizing this brunch as one of many "zones of ambiguity" (56) where critique becomes possible, Dew employs theory and action when she rehearses a proposal with several faculty and deans at the brunch and then finally appeals to the chancellor for help addressing low salaries and high faculty turnover. The actions taken at the meeting perform the conservative role of the WPA as a central "boss compositionist" who uses institutional authority to speak for all employees. Simultaneously, however, Dew satisfies the liberal call to "think differently" about conventions—such as the appropriate time and place where WPAs can make their arguments for better funding. Dew attributes such gains to "aligning our claims with the theoretical foundations and values that sustain our field" (58). Theory becomes a valuable tool to help WPAs attain pragmatic goals and to alter material conditions, not by combusting our conservative values through theory but by putting the two in sync.

Conclusion

It is tempting to say that WPA work has been theorized only in the last ten years, but my reading of prior articles shows that WPAs had theorized their position well beforehand. Such theorizing has simply gone unacknowledged because contemporary scholars have accepted as given the metadiscourse regarding WPA scholarship. My hope is that this reconsideration of the past three decades will encourage further use of theory as a valuable resource by situating it as a practice organic to administration, rather than a new development. We should certainly embrace Rose and Weiser's definition of a theory as "a way of conceptualizing, organizing, explaining, analyzing, reflecting on, and interpreting experiences and specialized knowledge gained through experience or observation" (*Researcher* 2). We should see this definition as inclusive of such theorists as Derrida, Foucault, Barthes, Bourdieu, and therefore accept their potential relevance to WPA work. However, we should resist the tendency to see theory exclusively as a dialogue with these figures. Work by Judith Butler or Susan Bordo can illuminate aspects of writing program administration, but that does not make them the best or only ways to theorize our situations. Even more importantly, we should recognize that WPA scholars have theorized administration and offered administrative theories of writing since the discipline's foundation thirty years ago. If we have been theorizing program administration for this long, then any allegedly conservative position against theorizing has no substance.

While administrators must theorize and have theorized, it is still worth recognizing a risk outlined by Gary Olson, who warns that if "theory becomes so capacious that it embraces everything," including WPA work, "then it no longer serves any descriptive purpose" (501). Olson cautions all scholars to exercise precision when defining the theoretical aspects of their research. While administration draws on theory as a guide for reflection and action, and can generate theories, administration itself is not theory. Olson's fear is that administrators might diminish their own uniqueness—and institutional value—in their rush to identify the similarities between their methodologies and those of other disciplines. Fortunately, the works discussed here avoid the pitfall of overly capacious terminology. They promote theories unique to writing program administration and possess an awareness that while administration is not itself theory it does, like any discipline, benefit from theoretical groundings of action.

To close, I would like to point out that Bruffee, even when advising against theory, does himself theorize WPA work as "inherently a boundary negotiating job" ("Thoughts" 62), which echoes cultural as well as poststructuralist theory's recognition of context and contingency. Bruffee goes on to say that "The boundary and the hyphen are where I believe the focal unity of writing program administration lies and what make it educationally and institutionally unique" (62), meaning that WPAs are always engaged in interdisciplinary efforts. WPA scholars have always theorized, sometimes even despite their intentions. The embrace of this intellectual practice means continued growth and change.

Works Cited

Adler-Kassner, Linda. *The Activist WPA: Changing the Stories about Writing and Writers*. Logan: Utah State UP, 2008. Print.

Atwill, Janet M. *Rhetoric Reclaimed: Aristotle and the Liberal Arts Tradition*. Ithaca: Cornell UP, 1998. Print.

Bishop, Wendy, and Gay Lynn Crossley. "Doing the Hokey Pokey? Why Writing Program Administrators' Job Conditions Don't Seem to Be Improving." *Freshman English News* 16.2 (1993): 46-59. Print.

Boyer, Ernest. *Scholarship Reconsidered: Priorities of the Professorate*. Princeton: Carnegie Foundation for the Advancement of Teaching, 1990. Print.

Bruffee, Kenneth. "The WPA as (Journal) Writer: What the Record Reveals." *WPA: Writing Program Administration* 9.2 (1985): 5-10. Print.

---. "Thoughts of a Fly on the Wall." *WPA: Writing Program Administration* 22.3 (1999): 55-64. Print.

Bullock, Richard H. Review of *Kitchen Cooks, Plate Twirlers, and Troubadours: Writing Program Administrators Tell Their Stories*, edited by Diana George, and *The Writing Program Administrator as Researcher: Inquiry in Action and Reflection*, edited by Shirley K. Weiser and Irwin Weiser. *CCC* 51.4 (2000): 672-76. Print.

---. "When Administration Becomes Scholarship: The Future of Writing Program Administration." *WPA: Writing Program Administration* 11.1-2 (1987): 13-18. Print.

Bushman, Donald. "The WPA as Pragmatist: Recasting 'Service' as 'Human Sciences.'" *WPA: Writing Program Administration* 23.1-2 (1999): 29-44. Print.

Coulter, Lauren Sewell. "Lean Mean Grading Machines? A Bourdieuian Reading of Novice Instructors in a Portfolio-Based Writing Program." *WPA: Writing Program Administration* 23.3 (2000): 33-49. Print.

Dew, Debra Frank. "WPA as Rhetor: Scholarly Production and the Difference a Discipline Makes." *CCC* 62.3 (2009): 50-62. Print.

Dobrin, Sidney. "Freedom and Safety, Space and Place: Locating the Critical WPA." *The Writing Program Interrupted: Making Space for Critical Discourse*. Ed. Donna Strickland and Jeanne Gunner. Portsmouth: Boynton/Cook Publishers, 2009. 56-72. Print.

Dunn, Thomas. "Writing in the Sciences." *WPA: Writing Program Administration* 4.1 (1980): 11-15. Print.

George, Diana, ed. *Kitchen Cooks, Plate Twirlers, and Troubadours: Writing Program Administrators Tell Their Stories*. Portsmouth: Boynton/Cook Publishers, 1999. Print.

Graban, Tarez Samra, and Kathleen J. Ryan. "From 'What Is' to 'What Is Possible': Theorizing Curricular Document Revision as In(ter)vention and Reform." *WPA: Writing Program Administration* 28.3 (Spring 2005): 113-16. Print.

Gracie, William. "Directing Freshman English: The Role of Administration in Freshman English Programs." *WPA: Writing Program Administration* 5.3 (1982): 21-24. Print.

Gunner, Jeanne. "A Needed Space for Critique in Historical Recovery." *Historical Studies of Writing Program Administration*. Ed. Barbara L'Eplattenier and Lisa Mastrangelo. West Lafayette: Parlor P, 2004. 263-78. Print.

Hult, Christine. "The Scholarship of Administration." *Theorizing and Enacting Difference: Resituating Writing Programs within the Academy*. Ed. Joseph Janangelo and Christine Hansen. Portsmouth: Boynton/Cook-Heinemann, 1997. 119-31. Print.

Kinneavy, James. *A Theory of Discourse.* New York: Norton, 1971. Print.

Larkin, Greg. "The Essential Unity of Language Arts Programs: Its Pedagogical Implications." *WPA: Writing Program Administration* 3.1 (1979): 25-28. Print.

L'Eplattenier, Barbara, and Lisa Mastrangelo, eds. *Historical Studies of Writing Program Administration: Individuals, Communities, and the Formation of a Discipline.* West Lafayette: Parlor P, 2004. Print.

Maimon, Elaine. "Writing in the Arts and Sciences: Getting Started and Gaining Momentum." *WPA: Writing Program Administration* 4.3 (1981): 9-13. Print.

McLeod, Susan H. *Writing Program Administration.* West Lafayette: Parlor P, 2007. Print.

Olson, Gary A. Review of *The Writing Program Administrator as Theorist: Making Knowledge Work*, edited by Shirley K. Rose and Irwin Weiser. *CCC* 54.3 (2003): 499-502. Print.

Olson, Gary A., and Joseph M. Moxley. "Directing Freshman Composition: The Limits of Authority." *CCC* 40.1 (1989): 51-60. Print.

Rice, Jeff. "Conservative Writing Program Administrators (WPAs)." *The Writing Program Interrupted: Making Space for Critical Discourse.* Ed. Donna Strickland and Jeanne Gunner. Portsmouth: Boynton/Cook Publishers, 2009. 1-14. Print.

Rose, Shirley K., and Irwin Weiser, eds. *The Writing Program Administrator as Researcher: Inquiry in Action and Reflection.* Portsmouth: Heinemann-Boynton/Cook, 1999. Print.

---. *The Writing Program Administrator as Theorist: Making Knowledge Work.* Portsmouth: Heinemann, 2002. Print.

---. "Theorizing Writing Program Theorizing." *The Writing Program Administrator as Theorist.* Portsmouth: Heinemann, 2002. 183-96. Print.

Sánchez, Raúl. *The Function of Theory in Composition Studies.* New York: SUNY P, 2005. Print.

Strickland, Donna, and Jeanne Gunner, eds. *The Writing Program Interrupted: Making Space for Critical Discourse.* Portsmouth: Boynton/Cook Publishers, 2009. Print.

Trimbur, John. "Introduction." *The Writing Program Interrupted: Making Space for Critical Discourse.* Ed. Donna Strickland and Jeanne Gunner. Portsmouth: Boynton/Cook Publishers, 2009. vii-x. Print.

---. "Students or Staff: Thoughts on the Use of Peer Tutors in Writing Centers." *WPA: Writing Program Administration* 7.1 (1983): 33-38. Print.

---. "'Writing and Undergraduate Education': A Report on the First Annul NEWPA Fall Meeting." *WPA: Writing Program Administration* 9.1-2 (1985): 59-61. Print.

Witte, Stephen, and Lester Faigley. *Evaluating College Writing Programs.* Carbondale: Southern Illinois UP, 1983. Print.

"So what are *we* working on?" Pronouns as a Way of Re-Examining Composing

Kate Pantelides and Mariaelena Bartesaghi

The encounters of writing center tutors and clients, this essay argues, are tensional, asymmetrical, and productive negotiations of a coauthored *we*. As authorship and authorization are discursive processes, we offer an empirical examination of how personal pronouns mark important shifts in the dynamic creation of a shared academic manuscript in writing center consultations. Though it is tempting to analyze the work of *we* as simply inclusive, our analysis proposes that *we* is multifunctional, periodically signaling collaborative affiliation and disaffiliation, marking the negotiation of coauthorship, implying shared identity, and acting as an indicator of institutional discourse.

The fictitious notion of the perfect writing consultant (who is neither too directive nor too hands-off) or perfect composition instructor seems to loom large—a destructive figure who inhabits the discourse of theory. He or she is an ideal whose invocation encourages a narrative of guilt that does not get told at the center of writing center scholarship, but remains at the periphery, whispered in conversations about praxis. Although empirical work lays bare ways in which writers and consultants negotiate work, authorship, and responsibility, the question remains how these behaviors should be construed. How can and should praxis be adapted? Can we do better at defining our expectations for this continuum of interaction for consultants and clients to alleviate the inevitable guilt that comes with the binary presented in literature?

To answer these questions and better understand the actual complexity of writing center collaboration—collaboration that is neither purely "peer," non-interventionist, nor authoritative, colluding expert—we approach the issue discursively, seeking to illuminate what lies between institutional discourse and interactional practice and to open up possibilities for an alternative discourse of praxis to take its place. We base our analysis on an empirical study of writing consultations over the course of a semester at a large RU/VH institution. The selections considered here are derived from ten writing consultations between graduate student consultants and graduate student clients at our university's writing center that were recorded and transcribed by the first author. The writing consultants are all MA and doctoral-level students from the English, World Languages, and Communication departments, and the clients are graduate students from across the disciplines. We find graduate student interaction analytically compelling, and the consultation serves as a privileged site for an exploration of their institutionally hybrid status, both with respect to each other and to the context that the consultation both invokes and (re)produces.

The encounters of writing center tutors and clients, this essay argues, are tensional, asymmetrical, and productive negotiations of a coauthored *we*. As authorship and authorization are discursive processes, we (also as coauthors) offer an empirical examination of how *we*, *I*, and *you*, mark important shifts in the consultants' and clients' dynamic creation of a shared academic manuscript. In analyzing coproduction and coauthorship, we do not, however, subscribe to the idea of *collaboration* as it presently appears in writing center and composition metadiscourse. We do not add to the robust literature where the term is evaluated as an activity which consultants (and ironically, for a term which includes two people, that is where the blame falls) in the writing center don't do *well* or could do much better or indeed engage in *badly*. By disengaging from the present view of collaboration, which has been part of writing centers since the work of scholars such as Stephen North and Jeff Brooks, we propose two things.

The first is to wrest praxis from the constant evaluative oscillation of writing center disciplinary terminology (i.e., good-bad, collaboration-collusion, symmetry-asymmetry, consultant or peer; see review of literature which follows) which can condemn or (more rarely) praise, but offers no lingo for productive analytical discussion, or transferal of a way to do things in terms of skills and bona fide strategies. What we offer in its place is an empirical examination of what it is that writing practitioners and writing center participants actually *do* when enacting the practice of composing. The second is to encourage a re-articulation, or a way to relanguage our doings—to an audience within and beyond the writing center itself—in a way that better represents and values the complexities of our work. *Collaboration* may serve well as an interpretive shell for a complex interactional sequence, but it is a gloss, and it does little to help us understand the dynamic itself.

A good place to start our examination of writing center discourse is with the figure of the consultant. As a primary character in writing center helping narratives, the writing consultant appears to clients and the university at large under several guises. Most writing center models oscillate between conceptualizing consultants as helpers in an authority dynamic structured in top-down fashion (Shamoon and Burns 140-48); we find them cast in various roles, as coaches, teachers, and even therapists (Harris 35-40). Conversely, consultants can be portrayed as cheerleaders on the sidelines (Brooks 2). Rarely are they presented as they are in practice—chameleons that change their colors dependent on the moment-by-moment discursive requirements of the consultation.

To add a new (dark) twist to this plot, a recent empirical study of writing center praxis argues that the relationship between consultants and client-writers is based on *collusion*, defined as a consultant-enacted, client-disempowering array of practices of "the same old authoritarian control"

(Lunsford qtd. in Rollins, Smith, and Westbrook 122), masquerading as collaboration. The critique might be renewed but its discursive backdrop is familiar. Indeed, the idea(l) of collaboration as "textual nonintervention" (Clark and Healy 36) has guided composition praxis in the writing center since North's 1984 treatise "The Idea of a Writing Center." In a relationship defined by helping, North drew a counterintuitive boundary between consultants' actions and writers' expectations, facilitation, and intervention. In a political relationship defined by helping, inscribed in helping discourse (see Edelman) where one party defines the terms in which what becomes known as help will be understood and delivered to the other (Bartesaghi 16), North drew an uncertain binary between peerdom and directiveness, writer's work and consultant's help. For, if as North saw it, consultants "are not here to serve, supplement, back up, complement, reinforce, or otherwise be defined by any external curriculum" (79), consultants' help is done by "talk[ing] to writers." However, despite North's subsequent willingness to reconsider his line in the sand (see North, "Revisiting"), not to mention others' arguments as to the complexities and practical impossibility of textual nonintervention in writing center interaction (see Ede and Lunsford), the existence of a "legitimate and illegitimate collaboration" discourse is, as Wittgenstein famously wrote, a picture that holds us captive (Clark and Healy 39). It is in our language, and our language repeats it to us, helps us reconstruct it, subscribe to it and, subsequently, even prescribe it.

Though we primarily refer to them as consultants and clients, thus choosing a metaphor from counseling of a various nature, writing center interlocutors in our data are both graduate students. They both orient to particular material realities within the academy,[1] and do so discursively. That is, graduate student-clients bring their writing to the center to ensure that they can speak the language of their respective academic discourse communities (see Berkenkotter and Ravotas), a linguistic accomplishment that most graduate writing consultants are also desperately trying to finesse. Both student-consultants and clients still struggle with many of the same issues that undergraduates do—meeting the requirements of assignments, structuring arguments, polishing manuscripts—but often these struggles are magnified, in writing theses and dissertations, developing IRB protocols, and trying to construct professional ethos. Because we propose to opt out of the binary that paints authority and collaboration as oppositional, we instead focus on the asymmetrical complexities that collaboration entails by examining how graduate student consultants and clients use pronouns when talking about composing.

Collaboration in Writing Center Practice: A Reconstruction

Within writing center studies, scholars have explored what collaboration entails by examining consultant-client discourse in terms of the dynamic of asymmetry implicit within helping relationships where "those who self-define as giving help set the parameters of the relationship defined as helping; within that relationship, helpers and helped have different access, rights, and duties in the negotiation of its terms" (Bartesaghi 16). In "Scaffolding in the Writing Center: A Microanalysis of an Experienced Tutor's Verbal and Nonverbal Tutoring Strategies," Isabelle Thompson defines scaffolding as strategies which "[support] students while they figure out answers for themselves" (423). She examines a "successful" tutorial in terms of the asymmetrical practices that take place in this interaction: direct instruction, cognitive scaffolding, and motivational scaffolding, signaled in both talk and gesture. Urging the writing center community to not mark directiveness as inherently problematic, Thompson cites its appropriate use as one of the most important facets of a successful tutorial. She writes that a student must be "motivationally ready ... [for] tutors [to] be productively directive. If tutors are too directive too early, before students are motivated to be active participants, the conference is not likely to be successful" (447).

Similarly, in her article "Dominance in Academic Writing Tutorials: Gender, Language Proficiency, and the Offering of Suggestions," Terese Thonus examines tutors' directives, accepting them as a natural and necessary part of writing center action, and she seeks to tie the strategies by which tutors enact dominance to gender and language ability. In her study of 16 consultations, she charts the frequency and type of suggestion as it correlates to gender and speakers' language status. While Thonus acknowledges that writing consultants' position within the institution provides them with shaky authority, she concludes that more than any other variable, institutional affiliation grants dominance most visibly (244).

As useful as Thompson's and Thonus's findings are, they intensify the metadiscursive disconnect between what we theorize and practice and *how we theorize what we practice.* Consider how writing centers employ the discourse of "collaboration" to situate themselves within their universities. A case in point is the authors' university writing center website, which characterizes writing center interaction in the following way:

> Writing Center consultations are fifty minutes long and begin at the top of each hour. Consultants do not offer proofreading or editing services; instead, sessions are conducted collaboratively, and consultants make suggestions to help writers develop their *own* work. ("Writing Center")

Such a preface leaves consultants and clients unsure of what the consultation will actually entail. What is the magical interaction that is not proofreading, not editing, but instead—appropriate collaboration?

Given this disconnect, it is up to consultants and clients to interpret and negotiate the meaning of "collaboration" in the moment-by-moment exchanges of the consultation as it occurs. In contrast to instructors, consultants' identities as collaborators are languaged in symmetrical terms; they are non-experts, non-evaluators, helpers that simply allow students to free themselves from writer's block. As graduate students helping other students—who are often going through the same milestones of university education—consultants occupy a hybrid "status that is equal yet somehow unequal" (Williams 38). Since writing center consultations usually begin with a discussion of the writer's project, the writer reading her work out loud, and then a move to Socratic discussion regarding what the writer would like to change, praxis can easily be construed as "textual nonintervention." But the idea(lization) of the consultant as a ventriloquist of sorts, who merely provides students access to their "voices," tricks consultants into being taken in by a (metadiscursive) Wittgensteinian picture that is incoherent with practice. And it tricks us, as writing center users and theorists, into imagining consultants as not actually doing anything other than enabling a process that pre-existed the consultation: a monologic vision which allows scripting of the very process and its characters. Discursive work adds actual voices to this monologue, suggesting that opting out of the picture is an empirical project, from the inside out.

Brooke Rollins, Trixie Smith, and Evelyn Westbrook explore the discourse of writing center praxis in terms of interactional ethos. In their study of graduate consultations, they examine how consultants use tools that, they argue, covertly deny authority: claiming ignorance, using embedded directives, and relying on the inclusive pronouns *we* and *us*. They write that:

> inclusive pronouns ... suggest that the client is actively involved in issuing directives. This use of inclusive pronouns is the most simplistic, yet perhaps most representative method of disguising the assistant's authority. ... For example, when an assistant uses the phrase "We decided..." rather than "I decided...," she insists that the decision is a joint one. (128)

Thus, for Rollins, Smith, and Westbrook, tutor contributions are directive, but covertly so: they are based on collusion. What is troubling about their analysis is that, by focusing on so-called tutor's authority, they do not take into account the dynamic, back-and-forth features of interaction, or how clients also use pronouns in the consultation.

We are interested in showing how in spoken discourse, or talk-in-interaction, pronouns reveal a speaker's positioning toward the topic at hand. This allows us to examine both the immediate context of the relationship of consultant and client and the broader frame of institutional discourse of composing within which this relationship takes place. In contrast, Communication scholars Kathleen Haspel and Karen Tracy have examined pronoun usage as a productive site for understanding speakers' strategies of affiliation and disaffiliation to what they are speaking about. In their examination of a disagreement at a school board meeting in "Marking and Shifting Lines in the Sand," the authors consider how varied the work of *we* and *they* can be. Alternately used as inclusive, disaffiliative, and accusative, Haspel and Tracy see how *we*, especially, is used by speakers to successfully claim a particular identity and strengthen their claims. Like Haspel and Tracy, our study values the insight pronoun use provides into discursive collaboration, and we use them to detail the nature of the asymmetrical relationship enacted within writing center consultations (as suggested by Thompson).

Discourse Analysis

In his recent contribution to *Composition Studies,* Paul Walker proposes discourse analysis as a method for reconstituting Composition's theoretical metavocabulary—terminology, enactment, and practical consequentiality. In also adopting a discursive approach, we continue Walker's reflexive move. As a method, DA involves recording, faithfully transcribing, and analyzing talk. An important metatheoretical assumption of this process of recording and transcription is that, though DA focuses on problematic communication settings, answers are not known ahead of time, but derived inductively from the data. Authority, or what is known in critical theory as power, is seen in DA as a dynamic of talk in interaction: it has to be claimed, and authorized, by participants in the talk, within a particular context. By focusing on clients' and consultants' use of pronouns, and their switches between the singular *I* to the inclusive *we,* our analysis emphasizes speakers' available resources (see Fairclough; Haspel and Tracy) for claiming singular and shared ownership of a text. Invoked by these claims are relationships of identity and responsibility which themselves speak of the discursive context of the consultation as helping interaction in an institutional setting. Our transcription notation is at an intermediate level of detail (see Gilewicz and Thonus); we capture pauses, simultaneous or overlapping speech, vocalizations, emphases, false starts, and non-verbal features of the interaction (see Appendix for transcription notation).

Analysis: Pronoun Use in Writing Center Interaction

In the sections that follow, we present four extracts from writing consultations to show how graduate students—as both consultants and clients in the writing center—avail themselves of pronouns to coproduce new meanings, a new textual composition, and reflexively share the work of composing. We offer this examination as an opening to set aside what is presently argued about collaboration and offer a way to reconsider it as a multifaceted interactional praxis along a continuum of asymmetric helping strategies.

We *as Influence*

As a practice which materializes and reformulates its institutional context, the writing center consultation is a dynamic of what Bazerman and Paradis define as influence, "a means of inducing or enrolling outsiders into an insider's view and commitments" (7). Pronouns influence by negotiating speaker's positions of insider and outsider as institutional members, or experts, raising questions of who may influence whom and whose commitments about the writing process are more important in an exchange. We illustrate this use of pronouns in an extract from a consultation, below, in which a graduate student client working on her dissertation in Education (G) meets with a graduate student writing consultant (T). Although G has decided to use the writing center throughout her dissertation process and she has scheduled appointments throughout the semester, this is one of her first consultations, as is made clear by her unawareness of writing center praxis:

Extract 1

55	G:	You don't have to read it like (.) you can read it quietly. I mean,
56		I've got other stuff that I can do.
57	T:	Well maybe what we can do is actually (.) to make sure that your
58		meaning and intentions are clear. So maybe I'll read the first ten lines out
59		[loud
60	G:	[O.K.
61	T:	And we can make sure we're on the same um (.) paycheck.

In line 57, the consultant uses *we* as a corrective response to the student's *I* and *you* presentation. Since the student has agreed to work on her project in the writing center but has not worked with a consultant before, she sets the terms of the helping relationship as one in which she and the consultant will take turns developing her work independently. His *we* reconstructs the student's terms within the appropriate institutional discourse of the consultation, reframing both the immediate praxis (i.e. how things will go) and inducting her into the discourse of writing center ideology.

In line 61, the consultant uses humor to mitigate his directive, encouraging the student to be on the same "paycheck" as opposed reading the work "quietly" to himself (Line 55); this deliberate use of *we* signals a "complex transformation, involving shifts of meaning and new perspectives," that asks the student to conceive of the helping relationship in a different way (Linell 148). Rather than simply signaling tutorial "collusion," the use of the inclusive pronoun functions as a creative way to induct the student into an institutional way of seeing and reconstructing the meaning of praxis from a client-led to a consultant-led dynamic. Instead of sitting idly by while the consultant does the work of the consultation, *we* invites the student to partake in writing center praxis, that of reading the paper out loud. The fact that the extract is sealed with an "OK" in a cooperative overlap (lines 59 and 60) suggests that the student accepts the consultant's invitation.

We *as Coauthorship*

Once they are presented to consultants at the writing center, client manuscripts become part of a cycle of talking and writing (see Labov and Fanshel) where the lines between suggestions for improvement and composing become blurred. This very tension, which involves the amount of responsibility toward the shared text, is signaled in consultants' strategies of affiliation and disaffiliation toward the manuscript they are working on with a client. Accordingly, *we* is used to signal the consultant's accountability toward the text as a shared, coauthored institutional product. Conversely, the consultant also shifts pronouns to distance himself from its coproduction and render the student accountable for it. As Haspel and Tracy argue, "In using a reference term, speakers state or imply their membership in one category (we) and, at the same time, their nonmembership in a contrast category (they)" (148). In the context of the charged school board meeting that they observe, Haspel and Tracy examine how a speaker begins his discussion by using *we* to "initially [position] himself as someone speaking on behalf of his wife and himself," and then soon turns to *they* when addressing the troublesome material at the center of the meeting (148-152). The following extract follows a similar pattern.

In this exchange, the pair is engaged in considering the client's response to an article. Since the client, a Higher Education MA student, is a frequent user of the Writing Center, she quickly recognizes the troublesome aspect of her request to work on a paper hours before it is due. From the outset, there is a tension between what the client (S) wants to work on and the consultant's (T) agenda for the paper.

Extract 2

16	T:	And when is this paper due?
17	S:	(4.0) ((laughter))
18	T:	Today?
19	S:	Today.
20	T:	To<u>day</u>? Oh my goodness. We'll see what we can do. Okay um.
21		What I'd like you to do (.)
22		You mind reading this out loud?

Notice how the consultant reacts to this common occurrence in the writing center: the challenge of an imminent deadline. He immediately introduces *we* in Line 20, signaling that the challenge of the due date might be something that they can confront together. In line 17, the student responds to the consultant's question about the deadline with a long pause and laughter, which signals her hesitation to introduce the troublesome material (see Jefferson). The trouble is reinforced by the consultant's correct guess that the paper is due "today" (line 18) and the student's emphatic repetition (line 19). In lines 20-21, the consultant orients to this trouble with an interesting pronominal switch, outlining the tension between what is doable and accountable as shared product and what is, instead, positioned individual academic accomplishment. In this short extract, pronouns already accomplish quite a bit of work, first signaling solidarity, then suggesting how the student is responsible for the work at hand.

The tutor reinforces the shared plan for the session in line 20 with "okay" and the subsequent vocalization "um." In this case, the discourse marker "okay" acts as a repair, that is, it allows the consultant to "take back" his prior version, in which he would be directly accountable for a paper "due today." Not finishing his utterance, he then switches to *I*, to do something he is solely accountable for. Here the singular pronoun marks the consultant's invocation of the ideological tenet of textual responsibility, where the student's role is to be solely responsible for the academic text and the consultant's role is not to intervene. Note, however, that this ideology can only be enacted by means of a clear directive on the consultant's part (line 21), though the additional backtrack in the following turn, "You mind?" hedges and mitigates the force of his instruction. This short extract encapsulates thirty seconds when the consultant oscillates between degrees of responsibility, demonstrating the complexities of working at the boundary of, and embodying, the liminal "equal yet somehow unequal" role.

We as Shared Identity

Whereas *we* may mark shifts in the helping asymmetry, it can also display clients' and consultants' co-orientation to the academic text as an emergent institutional product and their co-incumbent position as graduate students within the academy. Their orientation to a joint identity is exemplified in the following exchange between a graduate student consultant (T) and client (S), an MA student in Criminology, where the two are focused on the matter of correct APA citation. We present the beginning of the consultation (lines 1-3) and then move to a later segment of the exchange (lines 36-45) to continue our analysis.

Extract 3

1	T:	Okay, so what are we working on?
2	S:	Um, so we're looking at a paper for this course and she basically
3		suggested that everybody come, basically, you know for APA style
[[...]]		
36	T:	Alright, let's find those headings. They're all so weird.
37	S:	Yeah, I was just looking at the (website).
38	T:	Yeah, that's frustrating because it can be like really confusing. Because
39		you don't know [which to trust
40	S:	[Exactly
41	T:	Definitely. [That's no fun
42	S:	[((laughter))
43	T:	I think that's the right page, we've got seven different options there.
44		(10.0) ((read paper)) Okay
45		yeah (5.0) ((read paper))

    The consultant begins the interaction with an invitation to work on the task of correct citation together, beginning the dialogue with "What are we working on?" (line 1). The student accounts for her place in the writing center in an interesting way; by explaining that her professor encouraged "everyone" to come and that she just needs help on citation (lines 1-3), she modifies the consultant's *we* by making her professor responsible for her need to "work on" something. Additionally, she makes "everyone" part of the collective who needs writing center help and herself as needing assistance on APA style (line 3). The consultant's uptake of the client's response introduces a new grouping of *we* to the consultation: a "let's" (line 36), that includes the consultant and the client. This *we* marks a shared task between the two, which the consultant expands in the second part of her turn in line 36 regarding APA rules: "They are all so weird." With this small self-disclosure that reveals the consultant as also a graduate student miffed by APA citation, the tutor brings about a shift in the consultation. This is a discursive shift materialized in praxis, as we now see the pair engaged in reading the text together (an action not instructed by the consultant) and looking up information toward a common goal.

The consultant's additional contribution in line 38 illustrates how shared identity can be cultivated by graduate students working together in a collaborative asymmetry. The tutor's introduction of confusion and issues of "trust" (lines 38-39), with respect to information about correct citation, are direct claims of her identity as a novice or learner within the academic setting that she and her interlocutor occupy. The sincerity of this identity construction notwithstanding, we see by the client's overlapping speech in lines 40-41, and the laughter at the tutor's humor (line 42), that it functions as a bridge for the client to meet the consultant in a shared space.

We *as Marker of Institutional Discourse*

In this final example, the tutor (T) begins the consultation with the usual question, "what [are we] working on today?" (line 1). The student (J), an ELL doctoral student in Education, reads this question as a prompt for her writing center literacy narrative, describing her work with other writing consultants and the focus of her project in the writing center (lines 8-13). Although she answers the initial request for information with *I* (line 2-3), the client switches to *we* in her own narrative (line 12), signaling the coconstruction of discourse in the center and her knowledge of the writing center consultation as a specific genre of helping relationships, complete with expected writing center "talk" and requests. As Jessica Williams suggests, writing center interaction functions as a type of institutional discourse (37). Although it is distinct from "workplace talk," writing center discourse stands at the "intersection" of two types of institutional discourse, expert-client, as in commercial settings, and expert-novice, as in educational settings (39).

Extract 4

1   T: Ok, ((clears throat)) so what exactly is it we're working on today?

```
2    J:      I've been—I've been meeting for a couple of weeks with the other
             tutors.
3            I've been meeting many people really [((laughter))
4    T:                                           [((laughter))
5    J:      I've been working on this proposal and I almost submit
6            submit it next week (.) aaand I'm just trying to see what I can do.
7    T:      ((laughter))
8    J:      Definitely, I have limited time. I cannot really (2.0) uh (2.0) have
             fixed.
9            everything fixed. But for myself (.) I've told the other tutors.
10           I go to improve my writing skills, umm, I know that right now
11           I'm doing my dissertation, so uh, I'm just going to come
12           regularly here, so we will work on many other things (.) not only
             (2.0)
13           dissertation.
```

Initially, the student explains her goals for visiting the writing center, commenting that although she is now focusing on specific materials for her dissertation (line 11), she wants to improve her writing skills generally with regular visits to the center (lines 9-10). Through her narrative, the student displays knowledge of writing center philosophy and the idea of writing as a process. Her comments can be read as the student's acceptance of what she has come to know of the center; she has embraced the pervasive writing center maxim, "become a better writer, don't just produce a better paper." During the whole of the student's successful literacy narrative, the consultant agrees and laughs (lines 4 and 7) to affirm the student's acknowledgment of the particular relationship invited in the center.

In the four exchanges presented above, *we* is explored within a dynamic of talk-in-interaction, where both consultant and client strategies are taken into account. Our analysis shows that *we* and *I* have different functions in negotiating consultant and client goals within a *collaborative asymmetry*, a phrase that enables a both/and productivity for analyst and participants alike as they coconstruct the shifts and reformulations of an institutional helping relationship.

Conclusion: What Comes Next

Once the putative dichotomy of collaboration and authority is set aside, we are invited to opt out of its discourse and the relational terms that it prescribes for the praxis of composing. We may instead consider the ways in which a collaborative asymmetry involves a productive and creative tension between ideology and praxis, which participants both acknowledge and resist at will as they orient to each other, the text they both wish to improve upon, and the institutional context of the consultation. Though it is compelling to analyze the work of *we* as inclusive, and therefore a means for the consultant to encode so-called collaboration while, in fact, colluding, our analysis proposes that *we* is itself multifunctional: signaling collaborative affiliation and disaffiliation by sharing and distancing oneself from a text; marking the negotiation of coauthorship; implying shared identity by acknowledging a common status within the institution through the act of composing; and acting as an indicator of institutional discourse by acknowledging shared assumptions and constraints of the particular community. All these discursive acts embody collaboration, for collaboration itself consists of strategies of asymmetry by which writing consultants, as helpers in a dynamic, conduct interaction with their clients.

Our analyses, our critiques, and the metadiscourse of collaboration we have reconstructed in order to set aside here, do not remain in an epistemological bubble that floats separated from the ontology of our praxis. That which we define as "illegitimate" or "collusion," cannot but re-enter the conversations of our praxis as training, self-assessments, gossip and value judgments, affecting both clients and consultants. In the case of consultants, whose work the writing center depends on, we wonder what kind of resources this languaging of what is as opposed to what should be offers for them to build their own characterizations as professionals within the academy. Tutors either feel they are too non-directive and, as a result, frustrating in their suggestions to clients, or too directive, and thus misbehaving (see Pantelides; Blau and Hall) in their roles as helpers.[2] The frequent manifestation of tutor fear (Lidh 9) and anxiety (see Chandler), suggests that the discursive toolbox of "writing center orthodoxy" (Clark and Healy 36) could offer consultants more effective tools. If asymmetry is part and parcel of writing center collaboration (see Latterell; Thompson; Thonus; Rollins, Smith and Westbrook), as conversation scholars show that it is indeed a feature of any exchange (see Drew), then it should be an accepted part of the way writing centers present themselves outside of their own discourse community, to clients and to the university at large.

It may be that recognizing and detailing the kind of interaction that takes place in the writing center is not politically expedient. As opposed to the dubious words "coproduced" and "asymmetrical," and the fuzzy categories of what actual writing center interaction entails, the assertion that students develop "their own work" in the Writing Center is a non-threatening, symmetrical peer interaction that is much simpler and easier to defend to administrators focused on the dangers of plagiarism and academic dishonesty, especially those already suspicious of writing center work. Writing center administrators purposely simplify this relationship and define it in terms of what it isn't—a relationship with an expert, an editor, an instructor—in order to occupy a safe political space. Surely this argument has been made before, that writing centers must resist unfair university policies (see Kail and Trimbur; Clark and Healy; Grimm), but they've made this argument for different reasons, for institutional value change.

We hold, however, that a representation of writing center interaction as complex collaborative asymmetry is more in keeping with writing center ideology than playing passive defense, and eliminating the disconnect between practice and theory will help consultants feel more at ease with the requirements of their occupation. More broadly, Compositionists of all stripes can benefit from acknowledging the fuzziness of our roles and the lack of clear demarcation between who the university wants us to be, who we say we are, and what actually happens in classrooms. To acknowledge the discourses we enact in our relationships means to move away from the narrative of guilt that frequently plagues both our practice and our scholarship.

Appendix A: Transcription Notation

(.)	An audible pause, like drawing a breath
(.2)	A timed pause, in fraction of a second
[	Marks the beginning of overlapping or simultaneous speech
–	Speech that is abruptly cut off
(word)	Inaudible speech, with the transcriptionist's best guess between parentheses
((laugh))	Transcriptionist's rendition of non-phonetic material
Underline	Underline a word or part of a word marks emphasis

Notes

1. We thank one of our anonymous reviewers for pointing this out to us.
2. These are worries that numerous tutors have expressed to the first author in post-session discussions.

Works Cited

Bartesaghi, Mariaelena. "How the Therapist Does Authority: Six Strategies to Substitute Client Accounts in the Session." *Communication & Medicine* 6.1 (2009): 15-25. Print.

Bazerman, Charles, and James G. Paradis. *Textual Dynamics of the Professions: Historical and Contemporary Studies of Writing in Professional Communities*. Madison: U of Wisconsin P, 1991. Print.

Berkenkotter, Carol, and Doris Ravotas. "Genre as Tool in the Transmission of Practice Over Time and Across Professional Boundaries." *Mind, Culture, and Activity* 4.4 (1997): 256-74. Print.

Blau, Susan, and John Hall. "Guilt-Free Tutoring: Rethinking How We Tutor Non-Native-English Speaking Students." *Writing Center Journal* 23.1 (2002): 23-44. Print.

Brooks, Jeff. "Minimalist Tutoring: Making the Student Do All the Work." *Writing Lab Newsletter* 15.6 (1991): 1-4. Web. 1 Jan. 2011.

Clark, Irene L., and Dave Healy. "Are Writing Centers Ethical?" *WPA: Writing Program Administration* 20.1-2 (1996): 32-48. Print.

Chandler, Sally. "Fear, Teaching Composition, and Students' Discursive Choices: Re-thinking Connections Between Emotions and College Student Writing." *Composition Studies* 35.2 (2007): 53-70. Print.

Drew, Paul. "Asymmetries of Knowledge in Conversational Interaction." *Asymmetries in Dialogue*. Ed. Ivana Marková and Klaus Foppa. Hemel Hempstead: Harvester Wheatsheaf, 1991. 29-48. Print.

Ede, Lisa, and Andrea A. Lunsford. "Collaboration and Concepts of Authorship." *PMLA* 116.2 (2001): 354-69. Print.

Edelman, Murray. "The Political Language of the Helping Professions." *Politics & Society* 4.3 (1974): 295-310. Print.
Fairclough, Norman. *Language and Power*. London: Longman, 1989. Print.
Gilewicz, Magdalena, and Terese Thonus. "Close Vertical Transcription in Writing Center Training and Research." *The Writing Center Journal* 24.1 (2003): 25-50. Print.
Grimm, Nancy M. *Good Intentions: Writing Center Work for Postmodern Times*. Portsmouth: Boynton/Cook-Heinemann, 1999. Print.
Harris, Muriel. *Teaching One-to-One: The Writing Conference*. Urbana: NCTE, 1986. Print.
Haspel, Kathleen, and Karen Tracy. "Marking and Shifting Lines in the Sand." *The Prettier Doll: Rhetoric, Discourse, and Ordinary Democracy*. Ed. Karen Tracy, James P. McDaniel, and Bruce E. Gronbeck. Tuscaloosa: U of Alabama P, 2007. 142-75. Print.
Jefferson, Gail. "On the Organization of Laughter in Talk About Troubles." *Structures of Social Action: Studies in Conversation Analysis*. Ed. J. M. Atkinson and John Heritage. Cambridge: Cambridge UP, 1984. 346-69. Print.
Kail, Harvey, and John Trimbur. "The Politics of Peer Tutoring." *WPA: Writing Program Administration* 11.1 (1987): 5-12. Print.
Labov, William, and David Fanshel. *Therapeutic Discourse: Psychotherapy as Conversation*. New York: Academic P, 1977. Print.
Latterell, Catherine G. "Decentering Student-Centeredness: Rethinking Tutor Authority in the Writing Center." *Stories from the Center: Connecting Narrative and Theory in the Writing Center*. Ed. Lynn Craigue Briggs and Meg Woolbright. Urbana: NCTE, 2000. 104-20. Print.
Lidh, Todd M. "Nothing to Fear But Fear Itself." *The Writing Lab Newsletter* 17.4 (1992): 9. Web. 15 Jan. 2010.
Linell, Peter. "Discourse Across Boundaries: On Recontextualizations and the Blending of Voices in Professional Discourse." *Text* 18.2 (1998): 143-57. Print.
North, Stephen M. "The Idea of the Writing Center." *Landmark Essays on Writing Centers*. Ed. Christina Murphy and Joe Law. Davis: Hermagoras, 1995. 71-85. Print.
---. "Revisiting 'The Idea of a Writing Center.'" *The Writing Center Journal* 15.1 (Fall 1994): 7-19. Print.
Pantelides, Kate. "Invisible Expectations and Hidden Agendas: Behaving Badly in the Writing Center." Florida Regional Writing Center Conference. University of South Florida, Tampa. 17 April 2009. Conference Presentation.
Rollins, Brooke, Trixie D. Smith, and Evelyn Westbrook. "Collusion and Collaboration: Concealing Authority in the Writing Center." *(E)merging Identities: Graduate Students in the Writing Center*. Ed. Melissa Nicolas. Southland: Fountainhead P, 2008. 119-40. Print.
Shamoon, Linda K., and Deborah H. Burns. "A Critique of Pure Tutoring." *The Writing Center Journal* 15.2 (1995): 134-51. Print.
Thompson, Isabelle. "Scaffolding in the Writing Center: A Microanalysis of an Experienced Tutor's Verbal and Nonverbal Tutoring Strategies." *Written Communication* 26.4 (2009): 417-53. Print.
Thonus, Terese. "Dominance in Academic Writing Tutorials: Gender, Language Proficiency, and the Offering of Suggestions." *Discourse & Society* 10.2 (1999): 225-48. Web. 15 Jan. 2010.

Walker, Paul. "(Un)Earthing a Vocabulary of Values: A Discourse Analysis for Eco-composition." *Composition Studies* 38.1 (2010): 69-87. Web. 15 Jan. 2010.

Williams, Jessica. "Writing Center Interaction: Institutional Discourse and the Role of Peer Tutors." *Interlanguage Pragmatics: Exploring Institutional Talk*. Ed. Kathleen Bardovi-Harlig and Beverly Hartford. Mahwah: Lawrence Erlbaum, 2005. 37-65. Print.

Wittgenstein, Ludwig. *Philosophical Investigations*. Trans. G. E. M. Anscombe. New York: Blackwell, 1953. Print.

"Writing Center." University of South Florida, n.d. Web. 15 Jan. 2010.

Undergraduate Writing Majors and the Rhetoric of Professionalism

Christian Weisser and Laurie Grobman

> The authors draw on two surveys conducted in 2009-10 with graduates from the BA in Professional Writing at Penn State Berks, a branch campus of Penn State University. The surveys led the authors to understand a set of common attributes among our alumni (what they call a "rhetoric of professionalism") while at the same time problematizing the notion of an emerging "profession of writing." The authors hope the description and analysis of their two surveys will serve as a starting point for more detailed and comprehensive surveys nationwide, to learn more about the alumni of undergraduate writing majors.

[O]ur majors have afterlives. They leave us to become the major in action.

– Sidonie Smith (44)

Not long ago, undergraduate writing majors were a relatively unique phenomenon found at a handful of schools; today such programs thrive at large and small universities in every part of the United States. In fact, the past ten years might come to be defined as the "decade of the undergraduate writing major," for no other curricular movement within writing studies has proliferated at so rapid a pace. The CCCC Committee on the Major in Writing has documented this growth through a list of writing majors and tracks that numbered 45 institutions in 2005, increasing to 68 institutions in 2009—more than a dozen of which were brand new majors within that four-year period, and several of which have been revised to focus more directly upon the discipline of writing. As the Committee website suggests, this data demonstrates that "the number of writing majors is increasing rapidly, and writing studies is becoming more central with each revision" ("Committee").

This growth in the number of undergraduate writing majors has developed along with an increasing body of scholarship devoted to the subject. We see these conversations as part of a "first wave" of scholarship about the undergraduate writing major. In the late 1990s and early 2000s, scholars began to theorize and discuss the implications of undergraduate coursework in professional writing, technical writing, rhetoric, and other related curricular developments, some of which are markedly distinct from the traditional "English" major. Linda Shamoon et al.'s 2000 edited collection *Coming of Age: The Advanced Writing Curriculum* was among the first to call for an undergraduate writing curriculum separate from the literature major. Two years later, *A Field of Dreams: Independent Writing Programs and the Future of Composition Studies*, edited by Peggy O'Neill, Angela Crowe, and Larry W. Burton, advocated for independent writing programs while acknowledging the complexities and potential disadvantages of stand-alone status. At the same time, a renewed focus upon courses and programs in civic rhetoric began to emerge. David Fleming, among others, argued that we need to reconnect rhetorical education to "a complex and rewarding course of study" that develops a person who is "engaged, articulate, resourceful, sympathetic, civil" (172; See also Miller; Cushman; and Miller and Jackson).

Many see Kathleen Blake Yancey's 2004 CCCC Chair's Address as the impetus for more sustained and specific inquiries into the development of a discrete undergraduate major. Yancey's call for more scholarly attention to the writing major as a means to "begin to secure our position in the academy" became a focal point for a range of scholarly discussions about how, where, and why we should develop the major (321). Yancey's suggestion that we "have a moment" (297) in which we can develop an undergraduate major in the midst of the increasingly theory-grounded first-year, WAC, and graduate programs in rhetoric and composition has been heard, and an array of scholarly books and articles have appeared in the years following her address.

Many of the scholarly responses to this call focus upon the challenges and opportunities of curricular development, the emerging tensions between practice and theory, the expansion of civic rhetoric courses, and the politics of negotiating new academic territory. A special issue of *Composition Studies* in 2007 helped to further define the current development of writing majors and to "offer various cautionary tales, frames from which to consider developing majors, and possibilities for the future" (Estrem 12). Similarly, Greg Giberson and Thomas Moriarty's edited collection *What We Are Becoming: Developments in Undergraduate Writing Majors*, and Deborah Balzhiser and Susan McLeod's *CCC* article "The Undergraduate Writing Major: What Is It? What Should It Be?" extended the groundwork for the continued development of undergraduate writing majors. As Giberson and Moriarty write, this emerging body of work is important because it allows us to think about undergraduate writing programs in ways that "go beyond our particular circumstances, to theorize them in ways that secure their place on our campuses, and in our discipline, for years to come" ("Introduction" 7). Echoing this, Balzhiser and McLeod recognize that "our major is still defining itself" and that "a national conversation on this topic is in order" (416).

This essay begins the work of extending these first-wave scholarly conversations into the next phase. There are many important topics to be addressed as undergraduate writing majors proliferate and develop, including the ways such programs build interdisciplinary and intradisciplinary coalitions, the ways we define and name our programs, and the ways we might begin to assess and evaluate the effectiveness and quality of these programs. One important step toward the latter two goals is to examine the outcomes of undergraduate writing programs by studying the professional lives of our graduates. As the undergraduate writing major continues to expand, the alumni of those programs will have an increasing impact on writing-related professions and graduate programs. To better understand the ways in which their undergraduate programs shaped and influenced those alumni and how those alumni might re-shape and influence our programs, it is important to speak with them directly, through interviews, surveys, and questionnaires.

In the pages to follow, we describe a series of such discussions we had in 2009-10 with graduates from the BA in Professional Writing at Penn State Berks, a branch campus of a large university in the mid-Atlantic. As we will explain, the feedback and responses we received through two related surveys have led us to understand a set of common and noteworthy attributes among our alumni: their ability to gauge their audience, to employ effective rhetorical techniques and strategies, and to convey a sense of professionalism, ethics, and adaptability in workplace situations and contexts. This "rhetoric of professionalism," as we call it, is not exclusive to the alumni of our writing program (or to writing programs nationwide), yet we see a tangible connection between the rhetorically focused nature of our program and these alumni's ability to successfully navigate workplace environments. At the same time, our survey results problematize the notion of what we call an emerging "profession of writing," and we seek to understand and explain this trend by examining the disciplinary and professional contexts that shape (or fail to shape) our students' professional identities after they complete undergraduate writing degrees. We offer this description and analysis of our two surveys as a starting point for more detailed and comprehensive surveys nationwide that will help us to learn more about the alumni of undergraduate writing majors.

The Major in Professional Writing at Penn State Berks

The development of the Professional Writing Program at Penn State Berks is examined in "Why We Chose Rhetoric," published by Candace Spigelman and Laurie Grobman in the *Journal of Business and Technical Communication* in 2006. As Spigelman and Grobman suggest, our institution did not (and to date, does not) offer a BA in English, so the program and its curriculum do not internally compete with an English major for students, faculty, or resources, as is often the case with writing majors. However, this new curricular ground meant that there was little to build upon; nearly every aspect of the program needed to be framed, developed, and negotiated for the first time, often among faculty, administrators, and advisors who saw distinct ideological differences in what the program should be. Much of the tension revolved around the amount of theory to be implemented into the program's structure, course offerings, and course content. The article addresses the ways in which theory and practice were melded together in that program's initial curriculum, and it highlights the need for adaptability and flexibility in the continued growth of an undergraduate writing major.

Similar debates pervade the recent scholarship about undergraduate writing majors. In their analysis of 68 writing majors in 65 different institutions, Balzhiser and McLeod classify the majors into "two rough groups": the "liberal arts" and "professional/rhetorical" writing majors (418). Balzhiser and McLeod include in the "professional/rhetorical" category both technical writing and a "rather new sort of major, one that we have arbitrarily called 'rhetorical' in that the focus is certainly writing, but not technical writing," and that might more accurately be called "writing studies" majors (431). As the authors define the two groups, "Liberal Arts" majors have a predominance of courses in creative writing and literature, while writing theory and praxis dominate the "professional/rhetorical" majors (418). Dominic DelliCarpini offers a different method for classifying undergraduate writing majors, placing them on a continuum from praxis to gnosis. He suggests that programs range from practical and career-oriented, to liberal arts-focused, while some programs find a middle-ground and "explicitly keep one foot in each world" (16). Thus the program at Penn State Berks is what Balzhiser and McLeod call a "writing studies" major, and it is a mix of both gnosis and praxis, moving along the continuum DelliCarpini describes as we adapt to changing contexts, student populations, and scholarship.

These changing perspectives in the scholarship about undergraduate writing majors are to be expected; they are indicative of the development and growth of an emerging subject. Similarly, our Professional Writing major—like many of the undergraduate writing majors that have emerged in the past decade—has undergone continued reassessment, reevaluation, and transformation of its programmatic goals and objectives. In our program, we continue to strive for the proper balance of coursework in liberal arts, rhetorical theory, practical application, and other key areas. The initial challenges in determining the program's focus have not vanished; they continue to permeate all aspects of what we and other faculty have done as we have reshaped the program in both large and small ways. Thus the concept we call a "rhetoric of professionalism" that emerged from our survey is key to our understanding of how we have wedded the rhetorical and professional in our program.

The Professional Writing Major at Penn State Berks contains many of the features that are common among writing majors; therefore we believe that the findings of our surveys may be of interest to others who are creating or administer undergraduate writing majors. In addition to general education and other university requirements, our BA in Professional Writing consists of 39 credit hours. Similar to most undergraduate writing majors, our program's primary goal is to enable students to communicate effectively and ethically in a wide range of workplace and academic situations. The coursework is designed to combine "a strong liberal arts foundation with practical writing experience" in an effort to "give students a broad foundation in effective language use" ("BA in Professional Writing"). Students fulfill those 39 credit hours by completing five required courses in the major and by completing eight other courses in seven different categories—a total of thirteen courses in the major.

Prescribed Courses (15 credits)

Engl 211W	Introduction to Writing Studies
Engl 417	The Editorial Process
Engl 491	The Capstone in Professional Writing
Engl 495	Internship in Professional Writing
Engl 471	Rhetorical Traditions

Rhetorical Theory—Select 3 credits

Engl 472	Current Theories of Reading and Writing
Engl 473	Rhetorical Approaches to Discourse
Engl 474	Issues in Rhetoric and Composition

Writing for Publication—Select 3 credits

Comm 260W	News Writing and Reporting
Engl 215	Introduction to Article Writing

Workplace Writing—Select 3 credits

Engl 418	Advanced Technical Writing
Engl 419	Advanced Business Writing

Visual Design—Select 3 credits

Engl 420	Writing for the Web
Engl 480	Communication Design for Writers

Advertising and Public Relations—Select 3 credits

Comm 320	Introduction to Advertising
Comm 370	Public Relations

Creative Writing—Select 3 credits

Engl 212	Introduction to Fiction Writing
Engl 213	Introduction to Poetry Writing
Engl 415	Advanced Nonfiction

Additional Writing Courses—Select 6 credits (Courses can only count in one category)

In addition to all courses above, this category also includes the following courses:

Engl 110	Newspaper Practicum
Engl 250	Peer Tutoring
Engl 416	Science Writing
CAS 214W	Speech Writing
Engl 421	Advanced Expository Writing

Balzhiser and McLeod describe several features that are vital to a successful writing program, and which we identify as significant contributors to a rhetoric of professionalism through their balance of theory and practice, their emphasis on ethics, and their focus on preparing students for a wide-range of discursive situations. The first of these is a required introductory or "gateway" course, which Balzhiser and McLeod suggest is offered in just a few majors (418), though the trend toward such courses is increasing nationwide. Students in our *English 211W: Introduction to Writing Studies* examine writing not only as a skill one must master, but also as a complex object of study. The course exposes students to many of the central theories and subjects of writing studies, introduces them to key conversations in rhetoric and composition, and asks them to consider how these issues manifest in various professional contexts. These include, but are not limited to: authorship and ownership; writing processes; writing and ethics; writing history; writing and technology; and writing, race, class, and gender.

Just a handful of the undergraduate writing programs examined in Balzhiser and McLeod's study require coursework in rhetorical theory. Students in our program are required to complete at least two courses in rhetorical theory. One course is *English 471: Rhetorical Traditions*, which exposes students to the major traditions of rhetorical inquiry and their relevance to contemporary communication. Students also choose one other course that focuses upon rhetorical theory, such as *English 474: Issues in Rhetoric and Composition*. This course addresses contemporary rhetorical issues and subjects, and the theme varies from semester to semester.

As Balzhiser and McLeod point out, many undergraduate writing majors require an internship or a portfolio in a capstone course (428); our program goes one step further to offer these as two separate, required courses. *English 495: Internship in Professional Writing* and *English 491: The Capstone in Professional Writing* help to develop students' hands-on, practical abilities in written communication. Our internship course echoes Jennifer Bay's "applied course in rhetoric" (137), in that it combines regular class meetings, discussions, and reading assignments with internship fieldwork and contextualizes the internship through classroom discussion and rhetorical analysis. In similar fashion, our capstone course in the program focuses upon the application of students' rhetorical knowledge; its overall purpose is to provide students with the opportunity to reflect upon and integrate academic coursework, co-curricular activities, and internship experiences through the design and development of print and electronic professional portfolios.

Our program also has a rich *extracurriculum*, something Balzhiser and McLeod and other first-wave researchers have not yet discussed, but which we think is vital. The undergraduate writing major should provide students with opportunities to interact with writers outside of the academic setting and to apply their writerly knowledge in tangible ways. Many of our alumni have had the opportunity to serve as peer reviewers and proofreaders for

Young Scholars in Writing: Undergraduate Research in Writing and Rhetoric, an international undergraduate research journal. Some participated in our *Writing Fellows* program, in which they assisted faculty across disciplines with writing in their courses through workshops, peer-tutoring, and mini-lessons on writing related topics; writing fellows have also presented their research at scholarly conferences. Other students worked for our campus newspaper, earning credit hours while they wrote about important campus-wide issues and topics. The program's extracurriculum also exposed students to a range of other examples of public or "real-world" literacy, such as guest speakers who hold writing-related jobs, and bus trips to various literacy events. Most recently, students and faculty presented literacy-themed public displays and presentations together in support of NCTE's National Day on Writing.

Survey Findings

From its inception, the Professional Writing major at Penn State Berks has sought feedback from a wide range of constituents, including current and former students, faculty, administrators, and the public. To obtain this feedback, we have used assessment tools such as exit questionnaires, face-to-face group discussions, course evaluations, one-on-one discussions, and portfolio evaluations by community members. While some of this research was driven by our desire to improve our program, it was also shaped by our institution's assessment protocols. According to the Assessment Guidelines from the Penn State Berks Office of Planning, Research, and Assessment, "Each program is expected to implement at least one assessment measure annually and to produce a brief assessment report" ("Office of Planning"). Consequently, we were familiar with various data-collection strategies, and we drew upon our previous experience with assessment and upon the guidance of our institution's research programs as we began to develop a survey of our alumni in early 2009. We began our planning with a series of discussions with our campus' Office of Planning, Research, and Assessment (PRA), which helped us to design the survey questions and sequencing, consider methods to administer the survey, and later, discussed how to interpret the results. We were particularly interested in learning about the connections between our curriculum and our alumni's professional lives, and the PRA helped us to create a survey that would answer those questions. In fact, a portion of the research we conducted through this study was funded through an assessment grant from our PRA. At the same time, we worked with our university's Institutional Review Board to obtain human-subjects approval, ensuring that our survey would be ethical, unbiased, and responsible. We also relied upon our campus' Alumni Relations office to find contact information from those alumni with whom we'd lost contact. One of the things that we learned through this process was to use the resources available at our institution. We are not statisticians, and neither of us had extensive prior experience in administering surveys; the help of trained professionals in these fields was valuable to our research.

In summer 2009, having received Institutional Review Board approval, our alumni relations office gave us a list of the 67 graduates of the professional writing program.[1] Because the first class of alumni completed the BA in Professional Writing in Spring 2003, we had six years' worth of alumni in our potential survey pool.[2] We sent email invitations to this group through *SurveyMonkey*, a survey-hosting website. In the invitation, we explained the two-fold purpose of the survey: to learn more about our program's alumni and their professional employment and/or graduate school experiences for both internal program assessment and for research to be shared discipline-wide through conference presentations and publications.

A group of 29 alumni, including 17 males and 12 females, completed the survey, for a response rate of 43%. This response rate is considered sound for surveys solicited through e-mail (see Schuldt and Totten). However, due to the limited size of our potential pool of alumni and the overall number of respondents, our primary goal in this essay is to summarize and describe the information we gathered from our alumni, rather than to make inferences about a larger population. While we do draw conclusions based upon the responses we received, we do not suggest that our descriptions or analyses apply to all undergraduate writing program graduates, or even to those alumni of our program who did not complete the survey. As one reviewer of this essay suggests, it may be the case that "successful" alumni were more likely to respond, and that this may have influenced our findings. With that in mind, we acknowledge the limited basis of our study.

This first survey consisted of 42 questions divided into three categories.[3] The first category in the survey requested background and employment information, including questions about their current job or graduate school status, how they sought and found employment or a graduate program after completing their BA, and whether or not they were employed in a "writing-related" job. The second category asked further questions about the role of writing and rhetoric in their current profession or graduate program, focusing on the genres and types of writing required of them, their own strengths and weaknesses in these genres and types, and the degree to which our program prepared them for this professional or academic work. The final category solicited more specific feedback about their undergraduate experiences in our program. This category of questions was intended as a mechanism to help us assess strengths and weaknesses of various aspects of our curriculum, from the perspective of those who experienced it firsthand. The section also asked for feedback on how and why alumni chose the major, which courses and subjects have been most and least useful in their current professions, and what they learned through specific curricular and extracurricular activities. While many of the questions allowed for written comments, the survey was, on the whole, quantitatively based; most questions asked respondents to select a checkbox or radio button to provide feedback, giving them the option of adding additional written information with each question.

After carefully reviewing the statistical and numerical data, we were intrigued by our graduates' rhetorical savvy as they carved out their career paths, and we realized they had a great deal to teach us about their professional identities, their professions, their professionalization, and their rhetorical proficiency. As a result, we conducted a follow-up survey in the summer of 2010.[4] This survey, which also received IRB approval, consisted of questions that elicited longer, more descriptive responses. We asked sixteen questions on the follow-up survey, each of which stemmed from areas of inquiry we felt were broached in the first survey, yet were not explored in sufficient detail. For example, the follow-up survey asked questions about job searches and advancement, the alumnis' use of rhetoric in the workplace, their perspectives on professionalism and ethics, and their future career plans involving the profession of writing. There were twelve respondents to these follow-up questions (out of our original group of twenty-nine), and the written responses from this group were quite detailed, giving us greater insight into these alumnis' proficiency with rhetorical techniques and the ways in which they have employed a rhetoric of professionalism to advance and achieve their professional aspirations.

It is from our surveys that we have come to see this concept of a rhetoric of professionalism as common among these alumni of our undergraduate writing major. Their responses indicate a sophisticated understanding of what it takes to succeed in the professional world, and we see them collectively as part of an emerging profession of writing they and their counterparts across the nation are beginning to shape and define. Thus the rhetoric of professionalism involves both the emergent qualities in alumni of an undergraduate writing major, and also the ways in which these graduates may begin to construct a developing community of professional writers. As our survey suggests, these former students are effective communicators, rhetorically savvy, professionally focused, and ethically grounded. We identify several key features as part of this rhetoric of professionalism. First and most obvious, we see writing as a central focus of our alumnus' careers. Second, we note their ability to recognize and make effective rhetorical choices in the workplace. Finally, and perhaps most importantly, we see them operating with a clear sense of professionalism, combining expertise, responsibility, and ethics in their workplaces, yet without a clear sense of membership in a particular community of professional writers.

Writing as Central to Their Careers

It should come as no surprise that writing, communication, and related activities are central features of a rhetoric of professionalism. In our survey, 92.9% of our respondents suggested that writing was "extremely, very, or somewhat important" in their current professions—just 7.1% suggested that writing was "not very important" in their workplace. Despite the variations in majors that Balzhiser and McLeod describe, the basic commonality in these majors is a focus on writing, which understandably translates to a similar focus in the post-graduation workplace. However, what we did find surprising in our survey was the wide range of writing-related jobs, duties, and activities in which these alumni participate in those professions. Our respondents' job descriptions and duties did not fit into neat, preconceived categories, but were instead much more varied and wide-ranging than we had imagined. As the list below indicates, many of our alumni hold job titles that do not directly or indirectly mention writing or communication.

The students who reported being employed in writing-related positions hold these job titles (in their words, listed alphabetically):

> Administrative Assistant and Freelance Editor
> Assistant Manager - Business Development and Marketing
> Associate Editor
> Communications Director
> Community Habilitation Specialist
> Freelance Writer/SEO and Marketing Consultant
> Independent Correspondent for Hamburg Item
> Literacy Coordinator
> Marketing and Events Coordinator
> Material Systems Coordinator
> Project Leader
> Public Relations Department Marketing Assistant/Copywriter
> Reporter/Designer
> Senior Technical Writer/Editor
> Sports Correspondent
> Teacher
> Technical Engineer Writer
> Voice-over Production Specialist

This variety in job titles, coupled with the large percentage of respondents who listed writing as important in their careers, leads us to surmise that our undergraduate writing majors utilize their training in ways that we might not have imagined or anticipated. One strength of an undergraduate writing major is the adaptability of the skills and techniques that students learn through the curriculum, and we found that our respondents became adept at applying their training and expertise in writing and communication in a range of professions. We see a correlation between the diversity of our course offerings and the wide range of professions common among our graduates. This flexibility in the curriculum encourages students to think ahead about their future careers and likely accounts for some of the diversity in their professions.

Interestingly, we discovered an equally diverse range of job duties in our survey data. One intriguing aspect of our data was the verbs our alumni used to describe what they do: few respondents used the verb "write" to describe their primary duties; instead, many described a more interactive and authoritative type of communication as central to their professions.

Survey participants used verbs such as "organize," "develop," "monitor," "coordinate," "establish," "create," "synthesize," and "determine" to describe the types of writing-related activities in which they participate. While most respondents used these terms to describe some form of writing or communication, the word choices themselves indicate an emphasis on collaboration and responsibility as central to those duties. When seen in this light, communicative ability becomes a powerful tool in workplace success. At the same time, as we discuss later, the multiplicity of verbs complicates the idea of a "profession of writers."

We also found that our alumni respondents used a wide range of genres and techniques—often those not normally associated with their job titles or professions. We discovered that these alumni find writing to be central to their professional lives and employ a wide range of writing genres in their workplaces, though there is a clear shift away from traditional and print-based forms and toward electronic, new-media, and promotional forms of communication. Not surprisingly, email was the most common form of communication, with 85.7% of our respondents indicating that they wrote "frequent" emails. Online documents (such as websites, blogs, etc.) were the second most common, and 46.4% indicated that they wrote "frequent" online documents. The next most frequently-used genre selected in our survey was advertisements and promotional materials, at 28.6%. The fact that nearly one-third of our alumni write frequently in this genre might indicate the need for further curricular attention.

Our survey also found that other genres that are typically seen as staples of workplace communication and still included in many technical and business writing textbooks—such as memos and letters—were selected less frequently than we might have expected. We found that 57.2% of our alumni respondents write memos "rarely" or "not at all," while 46.4% said that they write letters "rarely" or "not at all." We believe that this indicates a shift away from traditional "printed" memos and letters and toward the use of email to communicate shorter messages. In other words, it is likely that these recent graduates use the electronic format (email) as their primary method for concise communication, and that they associate memos and letters with an outmoded print format.

We also discovered a low frequency with which these alumni indicated more traditional forms of writing. Just 10.7% of our respondents write essays with frequency, and 71.4% noted that they never use the essay genre. In a similar question, only 29.6% of respondents described the writing that they do in their profession as "thesis driven: focused on evidencing one or more key argument(s)." In short, we discovered that these alumni find writing to be central to their professional lives and employ a wide range of writing genres in their workplaces, though there is a clear shift away from traditional and print-based forms and toward electronic, new-media, and promotional forms of communication.

Our respondents' qualitative responses in the follow-up survey confirmed many of the statistical details from the first survey. These alumni were particularly adept at recognizing, contextualizing, and analyzing the role of writing, rhetoric, and communication in their professional lives. Several respondents described the wide range of positions available to trained writers. Angela, an early graduate from our program who has held a variety of writing-related positions, suggests that "There are SO many different types of writing jobs out there. But knowing how to write can get anyone a decent job, even in different fields." Jessie, who has held different promotions and advertising jobs, points out that writing is a "really broad field that has a lot of facets to explore." She goes on to suggest that "being able to write in itself is a highly marketable asset." Other respondents point to the relevance and applicability of a writing major in today's economic climate. Ben, a writer and editor with the Federal Register, states that "writing's focus on communication with different audiences enables me to understand and communicate extremely efficiently, a skill that is essential in many fields and careers." In similar fashion, Stephanie, a marketing assistant and copywriter for a regional hospital, indicates that "strong writing skills are an asset to any organization." While space prohibits us from including all of the comments here, many of these alumni made specific mention of the ways in which their communicative abilities have opened up diverse career paths and have enabled them to become successful professionals. As faculty and administrators develop and redesign undergraduate writing programs, they should consider the ways in which their curricular decisions will help to shape the professional choices of their graduates.

Rhetorical Awareness and Savvy

Among the most important traits of our alumni respondents is their rhetorical proficiency. As expected, most of these graduates state the importance of understanding audience and purpose in creating documents and in marketing themselves. As Mary, a marketing and events coordinator puts it, "You MUST know who your audience is to find the right rhetoric." Jason, a public relations specialist with an educational agency, tells us he uses rhetoric every day in his position "to advance the agendas of my organization and its programs." He is "mindful of the rhetorical implications" of the material he writes, especially given the diversity of the organization's constituencies.

Yet, we were also struck by these graduates' insights into the role of rhetoric in their careers. Stephanie, who works as a publications manager with a regional hospital, emphasized the importance of rhetoric in interviewing, asserting that being rhetorical is an "art" that includes written language and body language. Stephanie uses the term "diplomatic" to describe how she views herself as rhetorical: "I would go as far to say that diplomacy is a form of rhetoric. I use certain language when writing to entice community members to seek our health care services over the competition. I must be diplomatic in my actions while standing by my convictions." Jessie revealed that although she didn't have experience with fundraising, she knew *how to learn*: through reading, research, and asking questions. Matthew, a marketing and online content specialist, spoke about the need to "develop an angle," what he called "build[ing] a self-brand that makes you a desirable commodity." And several of our alumni, including Matthew, noted the need to go online: "Opportunities are there online, you just have to know how to seize them." Stephanie, in fact, has built on her full-time work with the hospital to write freelance articles on healthcare issues.

Our alumni's responses also revealed their adaptability to a difficult job market and their creativity in carving out career paths. We see them as *acting rhetorically*: working part-time or as volunteers until full-time positions opened up, taking advantage of unforeseen opportunities, marketing themselves on online sites such as *LinkedIn.com*, and creating their own opportunities for professional development. Mary volunteered for a non-profit Our Town Foundation in 2006 while still in college, and was hired there as a full-time Special Projects and Events Coordinator, where she stayed for almost four years. On *LinkedIn.com*, Mary stated, "The greatest lesson I learned in nearly ten years of consistent employment—through office management, peer tutoring, and now marketing coordination—is the need to be flexible." Ben did freelance reporting for a regional newspaper while searching for permanent employment. He has been with the Federal Register for more than three years. It does not surprise us that Ben, a veteran of the Iraq War, "tried to step up as a leader" in the various units of the Federal Register.

Laura, a communications director and creative writer who has been published in a number of different creative writing and literary journals, advises her peers to "Be prepared to look for work and to work in places where you never thought you would." Cortney, a technical writer for an engineering firm, pointed out that her job as a writer in the company is not secure, so she advises her fellow professional writers to always seek out opportunities and let others know the expertise you possess: "Be out looking for more work or projects to keep yourself busy and get to know more people in the company you're at," and "Don't become stationary and accept what they give you." Elizabeth responded that, "To advance professionally, I always interviewed a lot to find out what I wanted and what I didn't want. I also wasn't afraid to take risks and try things that may have been viewed as 'unconventional.'" Elizabeth markets herself on *LinkedIn.com* as an "energetic and driven marketing professional and talented writer who seeks to utilize her creative mind in a marketing, communications, or writing role. ... Success in winning business and producing high quality copy and collateral is attributed to Elizabeth's attention to detail, multitasking, and time management skills."

We also see a common denominator in these alumni's attention to technology. Several point to the ever-changing nature of communication technologies and the need to keep up with technological innovations, even if they are unable to seek formal training or education. Lynn created a website to teach herself website analytics and writing business and marketing plans. As she states, "I'm creating opportunities for myself and keeping my writing skills fresh while I do it." This ingenuity and drive is also displayed by Matthew, who, through various employment positions and self-motivated professional development strategies, has invented himself as a Search Engine Optimization (SEO), Marketing, and Online Content Specialist. His martial arts website, *Ikigaiway.com*, provides information but also "serves as a personal project in SEO and Online Content Development."

A Profession of Writers

Randy Brooks, Peiling Zhao, and Carmella Braniger assert that *"writing is a profession*, and ... students can gain entry into the profession as undergraduate students" (36, emphasis added). Our survey results both affirm and problematize this claim. The terms "profession" and "professional" may be defined in a variety of ways. A growing body of scholarship suggests that professionalism requires more than simple proficiency or skill, but also includes a sense of responsibility to the individuals and communities with whom the professional interacts. In their book *Good Work: When Excellence and Ethics Meet*, authors Howard Gardner, Mihaly Csikszentmihalyi, and William Damon suggest that ethical and responsible conduct are vital to many professions:

> People who do good work, in our sense of the term, are clearly skilled in one or more professional realms. At the same time, rather than merely following the money or fame alone, or choosing the path of least resistance when in conflict, they are thoughtful about their responsibilities and the implications of their work. (3)

Thus professionalism requires more than simple proficiency or skill, but also includes a sense of responsibility to the individuals and communities with whom the professional interacts. The authors go on to suggest that professionals "are concerned to act in a responsible fashion with respect toward their personal goals; their family, friends, peers and colleagues; their mission or sense of calling; the institutions with which they are affiliated; and lastly, the wider world" (3).

We see an important link between a rhetorically-focused undergraduate writing major and this emerging definition of a professional who embodies both expertise and ethical responsibility. In fact, this definition of professionalism reflects the curricular and programmatic debates that many undergraduate writing programs (our own included) have wrestled with as they've attempted to balance instruction in skills-based courses with ethically and rhetorically-grounded perspectives. This is part of a larger debate on the currency of our programs within English as a field, and even within the Liberal Arts in general. We find it fruitful for undergraduate writing majors to aim for alumni who do the type of "good work" implied by Gardner,

Csikszentmihalyi, and Damon, work which combines expertise, ethics, and responsibility. This rhetorical professionalism, as we see it, is not only the ability to make effective rhetorical choices in the job search and as an employee, and being verbally sophisticated and careful in written communication, but also, and significantly, being ethical, broad-minded, and considerate of other perspectives—all of those things we associate with both professionalism and with rhetoric. Like other majors that see ethics and professionalism as foundational, we hope that the undergraduate writing major will continue to develop these attributes as central to the curriculum.

Consequently, we were interested in whether or not these disciplinary definitions of the terms "profession" and "professionalism" were similar to our respondents' own definitions of the terms. Because these definitions are foundational to our program and curriculum, we sought to determine if these definitions had shaped or been redefined by them in their own professional realms. In our follow-up survey, we asked five open-ended questions to elicit their feedback about their definitions of "profession" and "professionalism." Most of the alumni who completed our survey identified personal integrity and responsibility as fundamental aspects of professionalism. When asked "How do you define professionalism?" our alumnus' responses varied according to their own duties and experiences in the workplace, yet many addressed the ethical dimensions of their work. Several respondents used the term "respect" as an integral part of professionalism. According to Angela, "Professionalism is maturity. Professionalism can earn one respect." Jason, a voice-over production specialist, points out that "to be professional, one must be respectful to everyone, regardless of position or stature. It means putting forth the effort to do the best job possible every time." Mary, a revitalization coordinator at a regional chamber of commerce, suggests that "professionalism is knowing that you have to maintain a respectful image to the right people. The image of professionalism must be adaptable to different groups of people: it's the ability to gain respect from everyone in whatever way necessary." And Elizabeth, a freelancer in marketing and public relations, states that "Professionalism is simply doing your job, as asked, in a timely manner and treating people with respect." Stephanie is able to "uphold the mission and values of [her] organization" while "truly believ[ing] in contributing to a healthier tomorrow through [her] work in health care." The responses clearly indicate that these alumni define professionalism as more than just proficiency and expertise in a subject area, but also as involving responsible behavior and personal integrity. Professionalism, for our alumni, requires a balance of expertise and ethical decision making.

Many of our respondents described specific instances in which their ethics were challenged in the workplace, and our survey reveals a group of individuals who apply their personal sense of ethics in their professional identities. In fact, these alumni had much to say about the ways in which their ethics influence the choices they make on the job; the questions we asked about ethics and professionalism drew lengthy, detailed responses from nearly every participant. Mary states that her current job often requires her to balance her "personal value system" and what is "right" with what she has been told to do and the need to "keep [her] job." Ben left one unit at the Federal Register because he felt his supervisor "continued to act unethically" by demanding more from her employees than she was willing to give and by precluding their professional development and promotions even when deserved. Jessie revealed that after two years in the development department of a local museum, she "did not really admire either of [her] bosses and some of their moral/ethical codes. And I thought if I had to become like them to succeed, it was unlikely that I would." She left her job as a result. Lynn is committed to a sense of right and wrong: "If I'm not comfortable with something ethically, I'm not going to do it and I'm going to explain my reasons for not doing it." She told us that she was fired from a job after confronting the owner of the company about ethical violations. She states further, "I have no regrets about confronting him and reporting him to the State Department." Angela, too, had to weigh her values with those of her supervisor at a small publishing/editing company. As Angela explains the situation, the supervisor insisted that the ending of a memoir be altered to improve the book: "That's HIGHLY inappropriate in my opinion, and while we debated over this dilemma, I had to leave my position in the end," since the book would have been marketed as a memoir even with a fictionalized ending. We were pleased to see this close connection between ethics and professionalism, as we believe this to be a central component of our undergraduate writing program.

However, while most respondents described themselves as professionals, fewer indicated that they felt themselves part of a "profession of writers." Some, like Lynn and Mary, give a mixed reply about whether they are part of a profession of writers. Lynn responds: "I'm not sure. Have I done extensive writing at all of my jobs out of college? Yes. Has that been the sole purpose of any of those jobs? No." Lynn is still "looking for fulfillment with [her] work, and it's taken a lot of swings and misses to get closer to that goal." Mary writes: "Yes and no. In [my current] job—writing plays a key role ... My goal in life is to find a profession, however, where I can 'feel' more like a writer." Other alumni seemed to apply a restricted definition of a "profession of writers," suggesting that membership in a profession of writers is dependent upon a writing-related job title or organizational focus. Stephanie, for instance, notes that she works with a lot of people "in Public Relations who don't exhibit strong writing skills," and that consequently, she is not part of a profession of writers. On the other hand, after several positions in marketing, Elizabeth is a freelance marketing/writing consultant, who states "I have never been happier with my career." Jason, who in his first job "was constantly asked to compromise my beliefs about quality and equity, and it made me miserable," is now in a position that involves "content creation, whether it takes the form of reportage, creative copy, conceptualization, or layout and design work." He tells us, "More than anything, I think I am viewed as a writer at work."

These mixed responses about membership in a profession of writers may result from several sources, including the belief that one must be called "a writer" to be part of the profession, and the diversity and variation of jobs that writing majors go on to take after graduation. Unlike other, more clearly-defined and delineated professions (such as "Speech Therapist" or "Civil Engineer"), job titles for writers often do not contain the word "writing" in them. Further, the types of jobs available to degreed writers can be more diverse and varied than those in other professions. These two combined aspects of the profession do not lend themselves toward a focused definition of what it means to be part of a profession of writers, despite the collective emergence of writing-related careers.

Another factor related to the ambiguity of a "profession of writing" is the variation in the names of undergraduate writing majors. Writing majors have developed under local conditions and exigencies, shaped by institutional types, institutional missions, the presence or absence of an English major, existing faculty specializations, and other material factors (see, among many others, Giberson et al.; Peeples, Rosinski, and Strickland; Scott). The names of those programs have developed with equal variation and diversity. This issue was a main topic of discussion at the CCCC 2011 Special Interest Group (SIG) and in the CCCC 2011 meeting of the Committee on the Undergraduate Major in Writing and Rhetoric. The consensus in both groups was that naming should remain as diverse as the programs themselves. Perhaps this conversation warrants further discussion about how naming impacts student and alumnus' professional identities, both within our programs and after they enter the professional world.

Future Directions

We have described and problematized three of the key features of a rhetoric of professionalism: the centrality of writing, rhetorical proficiency, and professionalism and integrity. Yet these are just a sampling of the attributes of our alumni respondents that were revealed through our surveys. The data we gathered through them is too voluminous to cover in greater detail here, and much of this is due to the contributions of these alumni. We have found this survey to be useful for our program, our faculty, and our former students. It has helped us to make important changes to our curriculum; to our gateway, internship, and capstone courses; to our extracurricular programs; to our understanding and continued questioning of writing as a profession; and perhaps most importantly, to how we communicate with and about the graduates of our major.

We believe our survey also suggests fruitful areas for further research. Perhaps a larger survey of the alumni of undergraduate writing majors nationwide might contribute to the development of the writing major as an established part of the academic curriculum, and we invite others to use our survey as a stepping stone to further studies. We identify several important areas for further alumni research:

- As we discovered, these alumni find writing to be central to their professional lives and employ a wide range of writing genres in their workplaces, but they are writing in electronic, new-media, and promotional forms of communication far more than traditional and print-based forms. If further research supports this finding, then curricula in writing programs may need to be reconsidered.
- As one of the reviewers of our original draft noted, the "meta-awareness" of these alumni may have implications for studies about the transfer of classroom writing skills to other contexts (see Downs and Wardle; Beaufort). Alumni surveys could provide more evidence about how writing instruction transfers to careers and contexts beyond the university, and we encourage researchers working in transfer studies to draw upon the voices and perspectives of alumni in their scholarship.
- A third area ripe for research has to do with ethics and undergraduate writing majors. According to William Sullivan, "To become a professional is to assume a civic as well as an economic identity. … Professionals must be seen to contribute to the public value for which the profession stands" (17-18). Our study precludes comparisons or contrasts to the development of ethics in other liberal arts majors, but perhaps further empirical and qualitative research may shed light on these issues.
- Finally, our survey and others like it suggest that we might want to reconsider the inconsistent naming of undergraduate writing majors. Jason Carabelli, an undergraduate in the Writing and Rhetoric major at Oakland University, spoke on this subject at CCCC 2011. Carabelli described a wide range of student perceptions in how student majors understand the discipline, attributing this in part to "the field's own contention in what it calls itself." Internally, consistent naming may ultimately draw more students to a writing major and continue to validate its legitimacy in higher education (see Howard, whose discussion is about undergraduate writing majors as public relations for writing). Doing so may also contribute to a greater sense of legitimacy and identity among graduates, as well as more consistency and recognition of those programs in the eyes of employers and graduate programs.

Acknowledgements

Though acknowledgements are generally listed in a footnote or endnote, we must mention our respondents' efforts here, since this article would not have been written without them. We were particularly struck by their enthusiasm and attentiveness in participating in this survey. Many of them expressed their appreciation at being invited to participate, others contributed important ideas that led to our follow-up survey, and some have followed our survey findings and the creation of this article with keen interest.

Near the conclusion of their article, Balzhiser and McLeod ask the question, "What do we want the outcomes of our writing major to be?" (430). Perhaps this survey, and others like it, may help to answer that question. The alumni of our various undergraduate writing majors have much to contribute to this emerging conversation, and drawing upon their direct experiences and expertise can be an important aspect of the next wave of research and scholarship about undergraduate writing majors and the emerging profession of writing. This survey might serve as a model for others who wish to assess the strengths and weaknesses of their writing majors through direct correspondence with their alumni. The undergraduate writing major may develop further by including students and graduates in the conversation, and the voices of our alumni and those of undergraduate researchers should play a direct role in that development.

Notes

1. The alumni relations office informed us that their records are very accurate although they might be missing one or two graduates.
2. Approximately 3,400 undergraduate students attend Penn State Berks. Since 1997 it has offered baccalaureate degrees independently from Penn State's campus, and it currently offers 15 undergraduate majors. The BA in Professional Writing is one of the mid-sized programs at Penn State Berks, averaging approximately 30-40 enrolled student majors per year over the past five years.
3. Available at http://berks.psu.edu/prowriting/2009Survey.pdf
4. Available at http://berks.psu.edu/prowriting/2010Survey.pdf

Works Cited

"BA in Professional Writing." Penn State Berks, n.d. Web. 22 Jan. 2012.

Balzhiser, Deborah and Susan H. McLeod. "The Undergraduate Writing Major: What Is It? What Should It Be?" *CCC* 61.3 (2010): 415-33. Print.

Bay, Jennifer. "Preparing Undergraduates for Careers: An Argument for the Internship Practicum." *College English* 69.2 (2006): 134-41. Print.

Beaufort, Anne. *College Writing and Beyond: A New Framework for University Writing Instruction*. Logan: Utah State UP, 2007. Print.

Brooks, Randy, Peiling Zhao, and Carmella Braniger. "Redefining the Undergraduate Writing Major: An Integrated Approach at a Small Comprehensive University." *What We Are Becoming: Developments in Undergraduate Writing Majors*. Ed. Greg Giberson and Thomas A. Moriarty. Salt Lake: U of Utah P, 2010. 32-49. Print.

Carabelli, Jason. "Undergraduate Writing Majors: Creating Space for New Voices." Conference on College Composition and Communication. Atlanta Marriott Marquis Hotel, Atlanta. 8 April 2011. Reading.

"Committee on the Major in Writing and Rhetoric (March 2013)." *CCCC*, n.d. Web. 30 May 2012.

Cushman, Ellen. "Beyond Specialization: The Public Intellectual, Outreach, and Rhetoric Education." *The Realms of Rhetoric: Inquiries into the Prospects for Rhetoric Education*. Ed. Deepika Bahri and Joseph Petraglia. Albany: SUNY P, 2003. 121-29. Print.

DelliCarpini, Dominic F. "Re-writing the Humanities: The Writing Major's Effect upon Undergraduate Studies in English Departments." *Composition Studies* 35.1 (2007): 15-36. Print.

Downs, Douglas, and Elizabeth Wardle. "Teaching about Writing, Righting Misconceptions: (Re)Envisioning 'First-Year Composition' as 'Introduction to Writing Studies.'" *CCC* 58.4 (2007): 552-84. Print.

Estrem, Heidi. "Growing Pains: The Writing Major in Composition and Rhetoric." *Composition Studies* 35.1 (2007): 11-14. Print.

Fleming, David. "Rhetoric as a Course of Study." *College English* 61.2 (1998): 169-91. Print.

Gardner, Howard, Mihaly Csikszentmihalyi, and William Damon. *Good Work: When Excellence and Ethics Meet*. New York: Basic Books, 2001. Print.

Giberson, Greg, and Thomas A. Moriarty. "Introduction: Forging Connections Among Undergraduate Writing Majors." *What We Are Becoming: Developments in Undergraduate Writing Majors*. Ed. Greg Giberson and Thomas A. Moriarty. Salt Lake: U of Utah P, 2010. 1-10. Print.

Giberson, Greg, and Thomas A. Moriarty, eds. *What We Are Becoming: Developments in Undergraduate Writing Majors*. Salt Lake: U of Utah P, 2010. Print.

Giberson, Greg, Lori Ostergaard, Jennifer Clary-Lemon, Jennifer Courtney, Kelly Kinney, and Brad Lucas. "A Changing Profession Changing a Discipline: Junior Faculty and the Undergraduate Major." *Composition Forum* 20 (2009): n. pag. Web. 20 May 2011.

Howard, Rebecca Moore. "Curricular Activism: The Writing Major as Counterdiscourse." *Composition Studies* 35.1 (2007): 41-52. Print.

Miller, Thomas P. "Rhetoric Within and Without Composition: Reimagining the Civic." *Coming of Age: The Advanced Writing Curriculum*. Ed. Linda K. Shamoon, Rebecca Moore Howard, Sandra Jamieson, and Robert A. Schwegler. Portsmouth: Heinemann Boynton/Cook, 2000. 32-41. Print.

Miller, Thomas P., and Brian Jackson. "Questions: What Are English Majors For?" *CCC* 58.4 (2007): 682-708. Print.

"Office of Planning, Research, and Assessment." Penn State Berks, n.d. Web. 22 Jan. 2012.

O'Neill, Peggy, Angela Crow, and Larry W. Burton, eds. *A Field of Dreams: Independent Writing Programs and the Future of Composition Studies*. Logan: Utah State UP, 2002. Print.

Peeples, Timothy, Paula Rosinski, and Michael Strickland. "*Chronos* and *Kairos*, Strategies and Tactics: The Case of Constructing Elon University's Professional Writing and Rhetoric Concentration." *Composition Studies* 35.1 (2007): 57-76. Print.

Schuldt, Barbara A., and Jeff W. Totten. "Electronic Mail versus Mail Survey Response Rates." *Marketing Research* 6 (1994): 36-39. Print.

Scott, Tony. "The Cart, the Horse, and the Road They are Driving Down: Thinking Ecologically about a New Writing Major." *Composition Studies* 35.1 (2007): 81-93. Print.

Shamoon, Linda K., Rebecca Moore Howard, Sandra Jamieson, and Robert A. Schwegler, eds. *Coming of Age: The Advanced Writing Curriculum*. Portsmouth: Heinemann-Boynton/Cook. 2000. Print.

Smith, Sidonie. "The English Major as Social Action." *ADE Bulletin* 149 (2010): 38-45. Print.

Spigelman, Candace, and Laurie Grobman. "Why We Chose Rhetoric: Necessity, Ethics, and the (Re)Making of a Professional Writing Program." *Journal of Business and Technical Communication* 20.1 (2006): 48-64. Print.

Sullivan, William M. "Can Professionalism Still Be A Viable Ethic?" *The Good Society* 13.1 (2004): 15-20. Print.

Yancey, Kathleen Blake. "Made Not Only in Words: Composition in a New Key." *CCC* 56.2 (2004): 297-328. Print.

An Emerging Model for Student Feedback: Electronic Distributed Evaluation

Beth Brunk-Chavez and Annette Arrigucci

In this article we address several issues and challenges that the evaluation of writing presents individual instructors and composition programs as a whole. We present electronic distributed evaluation, or EDE, as an emerging model for feedback on student writing and describe how it was integrated into our program's course redesign. Because the curriculum and delivery were significantly redesigned, the evaluation of students' work required reconsideration. The redesign opened a space for us to interrogate grading practices at the individual classroom/instructor level, at the programmatic level, and at a more theoretical level.

Even as Kathleen Blake Yancey observes a "fourth wave" of writing assessment emerging in 1999 ("Looking" 500), it seems that composition grading practices have changed very little in the past few decades.[1] While assessment theorists such as Bob Broad and Brian Huot encourage the development of local standards, and Yancey promotes assessment as a knowledge-making endeavor (484-85), grading in composition courses is not well understood and largely left to individual instructors to work out on their own. Concerns over instructor workload, fairness in assigning grades, and uniformity of grading standards are common for many composition programs. Moreover, even as online and/or hybrid courses have become permanent fixtures across the country, and as scholars such as Diane Penrod and Carl Whithaus put forth new frameworks for grading as composing moves into the twenty-first century, it seems many composition programs have yet to fully incorporate technology into grading.

In this article we address issues and challenges that the evaluation of writing presents individual instructors and composition programs as a whole. We will then present electronic distributed evaluation, or EDE, as an emerging model for feedback on student writing and describe how it was integrated into our program's course redesign.

Institutional Context of Course Redesign

Faced with a variety of challenges familiar to many composition programs—increasing enrollment; an "out-dated" curriculum; the preparation of graduate teaching assistants; and the retention of undergraduate students from their first to second year at the university—our composition program implemented a large-scale redesign, facilitated, in part, by the National Center for Academic Transformation and funded by a Texas Higher Education Coordinating Board grant. The redesign of English 1312, the second-semester first-year composition course, sought to meet Anne Beaufort's recommendation that writing courses should be "taught with an eye toward transfer of learning" (7), as well as to embody her five domains of process, rhetorical, genre, subject-matter, and discourse community knowledge (19). With assignments designed to incorporate each of these domains, students learn and practice strategies for a variety of writing contexts and discourse communities that they may encounter in the academy and in the workplace (9-12). In place of argument-based secondary research papers, students now work on projects such as a discourse community map, a comparative genre analysis, and a literature review and primary research report. To better equip students with the technological skills and strategies needed to communicate effectively, the redesign integrated digital literacies into the curriculum as well as the delivery. Digital projects include a collaborative documentary and an advocacy website, and all sections are taught as hybrids where students meet in class for 80 minutes once a week and complete the remainder of their work online.

Because the curriculum and delivery were significantly redesigned, the evaluation of students' work required reconsideration. The redesign opened a space for us to interrogate grading practices at the individual classroom/instructor level, at the programmatic level, and at a more theoretical level.

Issues with Evaluating Writing

Assessment theory has developed and changed significantly over the past 60 years, as Yancey, Edward M. White, Peter Elbow, Richard Haswell, Huot, and others have shown us. However, as Yancey also notes, for most colleges and universities little has changed with the long-standing model of writing assessment/evaluation in composition classrooms: "Our model of teaching composing ... (still) embodies the narrow and the singular in its emphasis on a primary and single human relationship: the writer in relation to the teacher" ("Made" 309). Yancey further describes the traditional model of delivery for composition courses as a "one-to-one tutorial model" where compositionists have sought to "reduce class size ... to conference with students, to respond vociferously to each student paper, and to understand that in our students' eyes we are the respondent who matters" (310). The labor-intensive nature of assessing student writing is one reason, among several, for keeping class sizes low.

Composition programs, however, are challenged to deliver the one-to-one tutorial model. From an administrative viewpoint, the tutorial model is expensive. While other first-year classes are taught in large lecture halls, composition programs struggle with the costs of hiring enough qualified instructors to keep courses within the 20 to 25 NCTE-recommended class size. While some predicted and cautioned that online learning would allow administrators to increase class sizes, it appears that while reducing the classroom space required, it has had little effect on course capacities, and rightly so when one instructor is still responsible for commenting on and evaluating the whole of students' writing.

A second challenge is that writing program administrators need to hire instructors who have composition backgrounds, yet programs often rely on teaching assistants and adjunct faculty who may not be well-prepared to teach writing. In "The Long Revolution in Composition," Anne Ruggles Gere voices what many have observed: "The teaching of composition is often entrusted to graduate students with little classroom experience or to literature specialists with no training in composition, and some departments still appoint as WPAs persons who have no expertise in composition" (128). Yancey observes that "the result of this staffing practice ... is that composition itself is too often not defined as the concepts, materials, and methods of a discipline" ("Delivering" 204). Instead, the courses may reflect the varied expertise, interests, and preferences of the individual instructors.

Third, issues such as grade inflation and instructor bias are concerns for instructors and WPAs. National data suggests that "grade inflation has been an issue in academia since the 1960s" (Rojstaczer and Healy). Reasons for this are many, and they include pressures to retain students, instructor attitudes, and "subjective and motivational factors" such as student improvement, effort, and persistence in the course (Schiming). Realizing that true objectivity is never attainable, compositionists often question the fairness of assigning grades to student writing. For example, a group of composition instructors acknowledge some of the issues underlying grade inflation in their 1998 article "The Conversation Continues: A Dialogue on Grade Inflation." Nick Carbone states:

> It's easy to see, now, that students would think effort was worth an A. ... Because the standards are different and difficult to explain sometimes, and because many teachers design courses where students are meant to succeed, not wash out, and because many teachers work extra hard at helping students do well, who regard students' lack of success as sometimes a teaching failure on their part, it's easy to see where the charges come from about grade inflation and low standards. (190)

In other words, the nature of many writing classes, and the attitudes of many instructors, lead students to believe that it's not entirely the quality of their work, but the extent of their efforts in the class that should earn them a successful grade. It's possible that this pedagogical approach can be detrimental for students who succeed in the class by trying hard rather than becoming competent in the coursework.

Beyond the general approach to the class, student grades may also be affected by instructors' individual perceptions of students. Melanie Sperling found that an experienced teacher she observed responded differently to students at different ability levels, creating different social experiences for each student (199). For example, to a student who enjoyed writing, the instructor showed herself as "positive, peer-like, and sympathetic" to the student's experience. To a student who was a non-native speaker of English, her comments were "negative, didactic, and focused on the mechanics of his text" (192). While Sperling does not negatively comment on the instructor's shifts in response, she writes that the data "raise questions regarding the relationship between classroom experience and student differences" (193). These findings point to the difficulty of treating each student equally when evaluating their writing.

Fourth, studies of student and instructor preparation for, as well as attitudes toward, commenting and assessment indicate that there is room for improvement in commenting and grading practices. In 1982, Nancy Sommers wrote that, "for the most part, teachers do not respond to student writing with the kind of thoughtful commentary which will help students to engage with the issues they are writing about or which will help them think about their purposes and goals in writing a specific text" (154). More recently, Maria O. Treglia notes the "contradictory and confusing" results of studies examining types of commentary made by L1 and L2 teachers. She finds that research not only reveals disagreement in response approaches but also leads some to question the usefulness of written commentary in general (68). Although her findings suggest that students' revision practices are more dependent on the writing task or revision suggested in the instructor's comment than the nature, or wording, of the comment, she also makes the important point that "what works for one student and instructor may not work in another context or between another teacher and student" (84). Therefore, instructors need to comment and evaluate writing in ways that help students succeed in any writing situation, not just their individual classes.

Compositionists have devised a range of solutions to mitigate these concerns. Jane Danielewicz and Peter Elbow propose contract grading, in which all students receive an agreed-upon minimum grade for completing certain criteria (246), as a way to "resist grade inflation" (252) and make grading less subjective to the preferences of the individual instructor (255). Additionally, data from studies on collaborative grading by George S. Peek, and Nedra Grogan and Donald A. Daiker, have shown that anonymous, collaborative grading is "more rigorous than the traditional method" (Peek 76) and tends to lower grades slightly, "between a third and half a grade" (Grogan and Daiker 29). Still, given these several challenges, it would stand to reason that students enrolled in different sections within one program would receive highly diverse educations in writing and would be evaluated quite differently depending on the background, interests, and experiences of the instructor. The instructors, however, are not to be blamed, as these hiring practices and lack of program cohesiveness have long been issues for many writing programs. Fred Kemp agrees that the challenges stem from a failure of administrators, "who are pretty good with ideas but maybe not so good at managing organizations" ("Computers" 106). We need to do a better job of turning composition theories into action at the programmatic level. EDE is our First-Year Composition program's attempt to acknowledge these challenges at the individual and the program level, devise solutions for these challenges, and put them into action.

EDE as an Emerging Model

As mentioned, the redesign of our curriculum and delivery required that our program reconsider our traditional grading practices because, in large part, "the changes wrought in writing with technology would produce different writing, and that different writing would call for different assessment methods" (Herrington, Hodgson, and Moran 204). We also desired to address systemic inefficiencies with grading practices that varied widely from course to course, tended toward grade inflation, and consumed a great amount of time for the instructors. Our redesign was committed to seeing that all students meet the same goals and objectives for the course, as well as to providing consistent high-quality and fair feedback on all projects. With a more rhetorically-informed curriculum, and one where students would be encouraged to publish their work, the program also sought to create an environment where students would learn to write for an unfamiliar audience rather than their singular instructor. Therefore, we sought a new model of evaluation.

Similarly faced with an increase in enrollment, the varied preparation and proficiencies of First-Year Composition students, as well as the reliance on graduate students as instructors, Texas Tech University created software called TOPIC[2] to implement distributed learning and assessment for its First-Year Composition courses in 1999, making it the first composition program to evaluate student writing using this method. According to Rebecca Rickly, a Texas Tech writing program administrator, the system has enabled First-Year Composition to be administered in a way that is in line with program goals. The courses provide "more and varied writing experiences," "timely, helpful feedback," and "frequent peer and self-critique" (191). She claims the curriculum is more "criteria-driven," and the program is "fiscally responsible" (193). She also notes that with TOPIC, students at Texas Tech receive a more uniform education across course sections because standardized criteria for each project are presented in class and then used by what Texas Tech calls "document instructors"—or graders—to assess the drafts and final versions of the projects (194). Finally, another benefit is an improvement in the quality of comments on and evaluation of student projects. Rickly finds that, "the criteria-based feedback [students] received clarified what was wrong and right with their writing and gave them focused, specific direction to improve" (194). Additionally, students can rate the quality of the feedback they receive, allowing for the continual improvement of the document instructors' work.

While Texas Tech laid the foundation for innovative approaches to the teaching and evaluation of student writing, our program thought it important to create a system organically, one that reflects our local program goals and challenges. Thus, eight months before piloting EDE, a collaborative of instructors drafted and revised what would become the common assignments of the program, the scoring guides used to evaluate students' projects, and the steps involved in the new grading system. We piloted 20 sections of the redesigned course in the first year. During this period, full-time lecturers and PhD students provided feedback and revised the course and its processes as needed. Over time, the program has settled on using EDE to evaluate four of the course's six major projects (and provide draft comments for two of these), for 70% of the grade. Instructors evaluate two major assignments, for the remaining 30%[3] and assign the final grade.

Although some of the details and sub-processes have changed as we continuously improve, the following steps have remained constant. On scheduled dates throughout the semester, students upload their drafts and final projects to a website that randomly distributes the submissions and makes them accessible to the graders. Before each commenting and evaluating cycle, a group of first-year graduate student teaching assistants (master's students studying rhetoric and writing studies, creative writing, and literature as well as rhetoric and composition PhD students), which we call "the committee," meets for at least two norming sessions. During these sessions, they discuss strategies for effective comments and scoring, review the assignment and scoring guide, read several student examples, and apply the scoring guide collectively and in small groups. They are also assigned to an experienced lecturer who provides individual feedback and answers specific questions throughout the cycle. The week before norming, the committee members observe the composition classes so that they have a strong sense of the work students are doing.

In summary, our version of EDE has the following features:

- Program-wide workshops provide both theoretical grounding and practical tips for teaching the common assignments.
- Instructors provide classroom instruction to students using common assignments.
- Students upload drafts and final projects (of most major assignments) to a website.
- Normed graders comment on, evaluate, and assign grades.
- One grader is randomly assigned each student's assignment.[4]
- Grading is done anonymously using program-generated rubrics.
- Students and instructors are able to access drafts, draft comments, final projects, and rubrics with scores and brief comments.
- Instructors assign end-of-semester grades.

Each part of the process is in continuous feedback and revision so that all parts of the process—students, instructors, and the committee—can work most efficiently and effectively.

Program Benefits of EDE

Five semesters into using EDE, the benefits to our students, instructors, and the program have become clear. Some were expected; others presented themselves over time. First, *instruction and grading became more uniform and less biased as students were assigned grades based on the quality of their writing according to a program standard rather than instructor preferences.* EDE helps us to combat what Rojstaczer and Healey describe as a lack of "transparency in the nature of grading in American colleges and universities. In its place," they suggest, "there is collective hearsay and conventional wisdom, and as is common with such pieces of information, this collective 'knowledge' is often completely wrong" (Rojstaczer and Healey). We suspect this was often the case for composition instructors in our program. Without education in grading practices and theories and an understanding of program goals and standards, many writing instructors are left with the "I know what a B is" approach to grading. The grading guides and the norming of the committee to those standards does a better job of creating transparency with grades and assures, as much as possible, that students across all sections are evaluated uniformly. Grade inflation is, in part, a result of bias,[5] and at our university, program-generated grade reports from the past several years have indicated that in some semesters, nearly 40% of students enrolled in traditional composition courses received A's as their final grade. While high quality work should certainly be reflected in the grade assigned, our program was concerned with the practice of awarding A's for B or C-level work, as well as passing students who had not yet achieved competency in the course.

As expected, we found that using EDE did show a different pattern of grade distribution than the traditional sections (see fig 1).

After the pilot year of the redesign,[6] the percentage of A's dropped from about 34% in the traditional course to 22% in the redesigned ones. B's have gone up, from 24% to 30%, and C's have gone down, from 15% to 13%. A simultaneous concern and expected outcome is the percentages of students who need to retake the course. There may be a variety of reasons for this. However, the slight increase in D's, from about 5% to 6%, may be attributed to fewer students being passed when they have not yet shown competency in the course. Rather than passing them along, retaking the course should better prepare these students for college-level writing and rhetoric projects. The number of F's and W's has also increased, and faculty development workshops continuously promote effective ways to keep students engaged and enrolled in the course. However, while EDE has a strong influence in the distribution of grades, we can't argue that it is the only reason for these changes: a more challenging curriculum and hybrid delivery also influences the grade ranges as well as institutional and personal influences.[7]

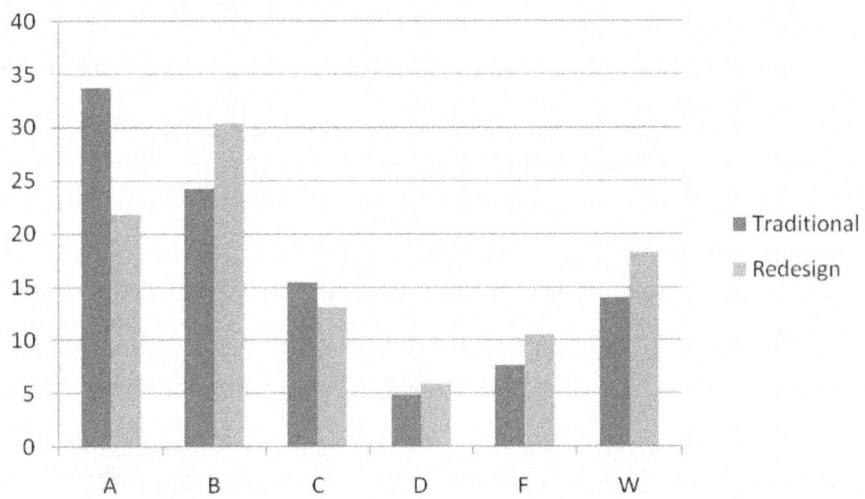

Fig. 1 Student grade distribution in traditional and redesigned sections, Fall 2008 through Fall 2010

Because EDE helps to minimize bias in grading, we wanted to know if students perceive the system as a fair grading process. In five semesters of survey responses, 20% of students said EDE was not fair; 80% of the students responded in the positive or were not sure[8] (see table 1).

Responses	Yes	Not sure	No
Students	59% (392)	21.3% (141)	19.7% (131)

Table 1, Student responses to the survey question: In general, do you think the grading system used this semester was fair?

In a focus group interview conducted during the first semester of the pilot program, 4 out of 5 students who participated said that using EDE was a good idea because it reduced instructor bias in grading based on personality.[9] Amanda said: "I thought it was good because it prevented instructor bias because sometimes when the instructor doesn't like you they don't grade accordingly." Another commented: "I do like that you have an unbiased party grading the final drafts because then the grading is very fair." Of those who reported that they thought EDE was unfair, most found it did not take into account student effort, which is largely measured through the relationships students build with their instructors. Students who commented negatively on the surveys made suggestions such as "the instructor should have more power in the grading system. The people who try hard and better themselves throughout the course should receive higher grades as well as those who already do [well]."

These student responses acknowledge that EDE evaluates the writing on its quality. However, they express a discontent with the fact that the committee members don't have immediate contact with students and therefore can't factor hard work, time spent, participation, eagerness, and attendance into their project grades. Rickly also reports that, with TOPIC, students can feel "disadvantaged by [their] lack of relationship with the teacher. Showing eagerness, being prepared, speaking out in class, and simply 'working hard' did not influence their grades, and many who had relied on these strategies in the past felt frustrated" (194). While some of that relationship, we are certain, still factors into the 30% of the final grade determined by instructors, students may experience frustration when submitting their projects throughout the semester.

A second benefit of EDE is that, *given the tight instructional budgets and the limited classroom space that many campuses are experiencing, EDE allowed us to increase our class size slightly without overburdening instructors with additional time spent commenting on and evaluating major projects.* Every fifth redesigned course allows us to save money on one part-time instructor and the space of one classroom.

Data from the three years prior to our redesign and the three years following indicate that the program has been successful at reducing our dependence on part-time instructors (which also allows us to be more selective) as well as the demand for classroom space, enabling us to schedule all sections in computer classrooms, an essential element for our redesigned curriculum. Taking into account the decrease in enrollment, the number of sections has been reduced by 17% for an average of 20 fewer sections per year (see table 2).

Years	Students/year	Sections/year
2008-2011	1943	65
2005-2008	2108	85

Table 2, Average students and class sections per academic year

Third, several accreditation agencies require that graduate student teaching assistants attain 18 hours of graduate credit before becoming the teacher of record for that discipline. Then students are funded for just one or two years of teaching thereafter. *With EDE, graduate student teaching assistants can acquire valuable and intensive hands-on experience by evaluating writing according to program standards before instructing in the classroom.* As a result, these TAs are well-prepared to teach a course that has a program-wide identity as indicated by common course goals, assignments, and evaluation. Kemp suggests that a composition program's high turnover rate, of something like 25% to 30% per year, leads to a faculty who is perpetually inexperienced. The result, he argues, is that little that is "very productive goes on in general education required classes taught by inexperienced teachers" ("Freshman Comp"). To complicate the situation more, many English department-funded TAs are not learning how to teach writing or studying composition theory in their graduate classes. Not only are some programs' teaching staff inexperienced, they may also be generally unprepared. EDE, through the work and training required to do it well, enables TAs to enter the classroom well-aware of the curriculum and program goals and well-prepared to teach writing. Long-time instructors can also be encouraged to participate in the evaluation process by working with the graders. As a result, all members of the First-Year Composition community are aware of, and deeply involved with, the program goals. Even if graduate students ultimately teach for just two semesters, EDE prepares them to do so.

In a survey of the graduate students who had worked on the committee and then moved on to teach, 100% agreed that the norming and grading processes helped them understand the goals and purposes of the FYC program.[10] When asked if the activities prepared them to teach, 70% said yes, 20% said no, and 10% were undecided. When asked if and how the norming and grading contributed to their understanding of the goals and purposes of our program, one TA responded: "Becoming more and more fluent with the assignments as well as what [the students] were/are working towards helped us to better understand not only the assignments, but what the students needed to understand in order to successfully complete the course." When asked if and how the TAs thought the grading process helped prepare them to teach the next year, another commented: "it familiarized my eye with diverse student writing. It also reminded me of the diverse cultures (and the styles of writing) I would encounter." Another reflected that "the grading process helped me get to know the assignments intimately. It also helped me to see the problems that arose for students in their writing, which allowed me to bring attention to those problems in class." Several also echoed one TA's comment that taking the time of "breaking down each assignment, looking at examples, and working out/debating why certain things were evaluated in specific ways helped me to then prepare my students to approach their assignments with these different criteria in mind." Although several TAs mentioned that they felt less prepared to teach the first-semester course (which does not use EDE[11]), one did acknowledge that the grading "allowed me to better prepare my 1311 students ... by knowing how students will be expected to effectively analyze and communicate ideas in the next semester." Few other training experiences could prepare TAs so well. Additionally, because the demand for part-time instructors is decreased and the savings have been reinvested into the graduate program, First-Year Composition has built a larger teaching assistant cohort (from 22 in fall 2008 to 30 in fall 2010). This strengthens our program because we are able to prepare instructors well rather than hiring part-time instructors who may not have experience teaching in the program.

A fourth benefit of EDE is that *the uniform curriculum and grading system allows us to make adjustments to the entire program's curriculum and delivery as needed.* Studies indicate that students are able to give valuable information on course effectiveness including "formative feedback to faculty for improving teaching, course content, and structure" (Chen and Hoshower 72). The feedback, however, is only valuable if teachers learn something from it, if teachers value the new information, if teachers understand how to make improvements, and finally, if teachers are motivated to make improvements (Centra 81). Because this feedback is collected at the program level, rather than from the individual instructor, the program is able to make informed, far-reaching changes. Small changes can be addressed in workshops and take effect immediately. Larger changes are compiled and published once a year in the local *Guide to First-Year Composition*. Instead of creating a *Guide* that attempts to address all the needs of different sections without, often, satisfying any, the program has created a valuable local textbook for our students and instructors. Susan Lang similarly notes that at Texas Tech "the program has evolved into a fluid, dynamic model of networked learning. Program administrators can make adjustments to improve the experience based on information collected and analyzed from ... multiple feedback loops" (558). In addition to a more profound understanding of students' strengths and weaknesses, we continuously measure the effect of the evaluation process with online surveys for students, TAs, and instructors, as well as with student focus groups. In these ways, EDE is an ever-evolving project informed by wide-ranging data.

A fifth benefit is that EDE *allows instructors to invest additional time in developing and revising the curriculum and instruction as well as in coaching their students on their writing projects.* Although their work addresses grading contracts, Danielwicz and Elbow make a point that resonates with EDE:

> our main goal is a system that can help teachers and students ... who want to think more about writing and less about grades. Our immediate goal is to put more energy into figuring out which activities most reliably produce learning, and less energy into figuring out a numerical grade for a piece of writing. (249)

Because our program was engaged in a wholesale redesign, the experienced instructors used the time that they would normally spend on grading and invested that into creating and improving the in-class and online scaffolding for assignments. New instructors, such as the graduate students entering the classroom, spend more time preparing and planning for effective face-to-face and online instruction. Instructors report that they dedicate more time to helping students learn effective technology applications and strategies for their projects. Additionally, instructors are able to focus more on responding to students' questions, drafts, and concerns. In an interview, one instructor reports feeling like she "can spend more time on the composing process, on getting students from invention to final projects," than when she was spending her time grading the previous assignment. Instead of focusing on those individual grades, instructors teaching with EDE can take a more holistic view of the writing goals students achieve and then focus on the ones with which students need more assistance.

Finally, *EDE emphasizes to students that they are not writing for a singular, known teacher, but they are composing for an audience who doesn't know their personalities, their class attendance, or their efforts.* EDE forces students to recognize and write with a larger audience in mind, thereby widening the rhetorical path for their work. While instructors sometimes suggest that students imagine different audiences for the assignments, it can be confusing to students when their instructor is still the audience who will assign a grade. While EDE doesn't expand the audience beyond the academic/graded sense (there is still a specific assignment, with a specific rubric, and a specific group who will grade the project), it does push the boundaries beyond the one-to-one model. Additionally, because students will produce a documentary and a website that can be shown at a public event and/or published to the internet, practicing writing to an unknown audience prepares them for these rhetorical tasks.

When students know their instructor will not be evaluating the projects, they can't as easily trap themselves into the "just tell me what I need to do for an A" mentality, but need to instead focus on writing effectively for an unknown audience. Some students have suggested that writing for someone other than their instructor is a scary thing, but others have found confidence in the effectiveness of their writing by following the program-created guidelines for projects, attending class regularly, taking feedback from their peers and instructors, and being tutored at the University Writing Center.

Questions, Critiques, and Concerns

These several benefits have improved our program in specific and far-reaching ways. However, not every First-Year Composition program would experience the same results. In fact, many instructors, scholars, and administrators may have a difficult time imagining that EDE is an effective method for teaching writing and running a program. We contend that many have cast a critical eye on EDE because the model so radically challenges long-held assumptions that inform the way composition courses are taught. We agree that such a radical change deserves careful consideration, and its implications should be fully explored. In this section, we will consider several concerns and the extent to which we have been able to address them in our program.

When we first proposed applying for the Texas Higher Education Coordinating Board grant that would support this redesign, several of our long-term instructors experienced what Kemp calls "the psychology of loss" ("Computers" 108). They were shocked, understandably, at the idea of separating instruction from evaluation in a composition class. One significant concern was whether using EDE would diminish or remove instructor's authority. If grades play the role of reward or punishment, what would instructors be able to use in their place? How would instructors connect with their students otherwise? In "A New Way to Grade," published in the *Chronicle of Higher Education* in 2006, Paula Wasley similarly reports that the most common complaint of Texas Tech graduate student instructors was that "the system erodes their authority and autonomy as teachers" (A6). Some instructors were dismayed that they could not reward with higher grades those students who showed effort in class. So, for our program directors, this fundamental shift required discussing the theoretical, pedagogical, and practical reasons informing the change, as some instructors believed they were "in trouble" or weren't trusted to evaluate their students fairly. To strike a balance, we decided to have instructors evaluate 30% of the students' work and also be responsible for calculating, determining, and submitting final grades. We have found that this arrangement has worked very well. Instructors are still responsible for the final decision, but that final decision is informed through a variety of measures.

Another concern is that once into the process, some instructors feel that the common curriculum, with its program-wide due dates, does not allow for flexibility and makes the semester feel "grade-driven" as the goal becomes getting the students to submit their work by the due dates. (Of course, this concern also exists in programs that have common assignments and due dates but do not use EDE.) Again, our program has adapted by creating submission windows that are open for several days and by varying possibilities for feedback in the drafting stages. Instructors are encouraged to think less about the final submission and more about the instruction that students need to move through their writing processes. They are also encouraged, though, to keep their students on track and avoid situations where students are behind in their submission.[12]

Michael Knievel raises questions about the delivery of grades based on his experience working with TOPIC at Texas Tech. In his 2001 *Kairos* web text "Gauging the Value of Online Grade Posting: An Inquiry into Full Disclosure," Knievel wonders if issuing grades online—or outside of the immediate context of the classroom—suggests to students that the grades are static and not open for discussion. "The grade has a feeling of fixedness, of being already decided, added to the average and backed by the legitimating force of technology." He therefore privileges "the immediacy of face-to-face grade disclosure" (Knievel).

We suggest that this notion of grade negotiation creates an unfair system as not all students are comfortable negotiating grades with their instructor. However, we recognize that there will be times when a project does require another look, and created in the program a "grade review" process in which students must articulate clearly why their project deserves a better grade. Effort and tutoring at the Writing Center are not valid reasons.

Instead, students must review their project according to the scoring guide and articulate why their grade is not reflective of their project's quality. Again, because the review is not handled by the individual instructor, but by a grade review committee, the student can feel more comfortable with the request and will likely receive a more fair assessment. Additionally, it diminishes the advantage that those bolder students hold over the ones who accept their grade, whether it's delivered in class or online.

Given that using EDE is unlike what students had experienced in their previous composition classes, many critics' first response is "students will hate this." However, we were surprised to see that the number of requests for a return to the traditional model was relatively small and that students indicated general satisfaction with the system. Of the students who responded to our surveys over the last five semesters, 53.3% were satisfied or very satisfied, and 22% were neutral. This indicates that less than a quarter of the students responding to the survey were dissatisfied (see table 3).

Responses	Very dissatisfied	Dissatisfied	Neither satisfied nor dissatisfied	Satisfied	Very satisfied
Students	9.4% (62)	15% (99)	22.3% (147)	41.7% (275)	11.6% (76)

Table 3, Student responses to the survey question: How satisfied were you with the grading system used in the English 1312 course?

Students in the focus groups generally felt that they were more on their own with keeping track of assignments and grades. "You have to (be) more responsible because you have to look at your comments and be more independent," Miguel said. Similarly, several students in focus groups suggested that EDE created a different relationship with their instructor. They saw their instructor more as a resource than as an evaluator. They reported emailing their instructor more frequently to ask questions and/or visiting the Writing Center often. Otherwise, most found that it didn't change their relationship with their instructor. "[It] didn't change my interaction with the teacher ... I was in the Writing Center a lot and so was the professor. He really helped shape drafts," Marcus said.

However, students do have some justifiable concerns with EDE. Some notice a disconnect between what they learn in class and what is emphasized in the evaluation phase. One student commented: "They do not know what goes on in our class, so that's probably why they grade extremely hard." Students may also find a difference in the comments they receive on drafts and then the graded project. One focus group student says: "The comments I received on the rough draft were excellent. What was commented was that it was an 'A' paper that only needed minor corrections. I was thrilled and so I corrected my paper and submitted with confidence. When I got the final grade

I was more confused than upset when I received a 'C'." In these instances, students won't see the draft feedback as valuable because the motivation for submitting drafts is primarily to get a better grade on the final project. The program uses this feedback from students to revise rubrics, improve the committee's norming sessions, and encourage more thoughtful feedback.[13]

On a more theoretical level, Catherine Gouge, in "Conversations at a Crucial Moment," criticizes Texas Tech's characterization of EDE as "objective" and argues that any such claims "challenge much current assessment theory" because "subjectivity in assessment is unavoidable" given that readers bring their own values to a reading and evaluation of a text (351). Even evaluation according to a rubric reveals a certain bias according to the instructor or program which created it. Gouge also states that using this system "to deny students to the subjectivities of their evaluators does not ensure objectivity in evaluation—it simply denies students access to the more experienced writer-subjects who are responding to their writing" (356). Gouge disagrees that assessment and evaluation, to be valid, must be anonymous (356) and contends that distributed grading "denies [students] access to what could be an innovative intersubjective writing-feeback process" (356). There certainly are contexts where it is important for students to have access to, and to feel a personal connection with, the person who is evaluating their work. However, we argue that First-Year Composition courses, particularly the second-semester courses, can be improved by urging students to envision an audience beyond their instructor. While some students may well want to sit with the person who evaluated their project, alternatives such as their instructor or a tutor at the Writing Center are also good sources of feedback. In other words, the students do not necessarily suffer from this "denial of access."

Conclusion

The questions, concerns, and critiques against EDE are valid for a number of reasons. However, our experiences and willingness to continuously review and revise have made the shift a worthwhile effort and have resulted in a stronger First-Year Composition program. We argue that EDE creates a program-level system that creates greater transparency for students, instructors, and administrators, as well as creating a program that can more effectively reflect on and improve itself. We believe our results with grade data, student and graduate student perception, space and money saved, as well as continuous improvement of the program, demonstrate that EDE is a viable option for grading in First-Year Composition programs, particularly at large public universities with graduate programs.

Notes

1. The data in this article was collected under IRB approval from the University of Texas at El Paso: Study #80228-1 Analyzing Student Attitudes Toward Online

Hybrid Classes and Study #92452-5 Study on Second-Semester Composition Course Redesign.
2. TOPIC stands for Texas Tech Online/Print Integrated Curriculum. Its second version is called ICON (Interactive Composition Online).
3. The 30% graded by the instructors includes a presentation and an advocacy website as well as other projects that the instructor wishes to assign.
4. Unlike Texas Tech, which uses two graders per project, we have only been able to use one grader. However, during the fall semester, when the number of students enrolled is not as high in 1312 as the spring, we have asked committee members to double score projects to determine if the grades are significantly different between graders and then make adjustments to the norming if needed. The EDE team helps to determine if the original score can stand or if the score needs to be revised. This process not only provides the opportunity to provide fair evaluations of the students' work, but it also provides additional opportunity for helping those graduate students who may need a bit more assistance with the evaluation process.
5. Bias can manifest itself in a variety of ways, both positively and negatively for students. Schiming includes: attention to the personal issues of students, use of "subjective or motivational factors," and faculty attitudes.
6. The traditional course grade data in this chart and described here is from Fall 2005 through Spring 2009. The redesigned course grade data is from Fall 2009 through Fall 2010. After Spring 2009, no traditional sections were offered. Redesign pilot grade data is excluded from this chart.
7. Continued studies in this area will demonstrate the complexity of grades and the challenges of evaluating impacts on grade distribution. While we find our results to be significant in these first few years of using EDE, extended data analysis is required for a more definitive conclusion.
8. Students were asked to participate in online surveys after submitting their second major project and at the end of the semester. The results are taken from the end-of-semester surveys. From Fall 2008 to Fall 2010, 928 students participated in this survey. Participation was voluntary, though instructors did offer extra credit points to students who participated.
9. We should note that students volunteered for the interviews, so the students are not a representative section of all students in the course. Student names have been changed to protect their identities.
10. In Fall 2010, 16 First-Year Composition graduate students responded to this survey.
11. We do not use EDE in the first-semester course primarily because we do not have enough graduate teaching assistants to support the work load of evaluating those assignments as well.
12. One concern that must be addressed every semester is what happens when students don't submit their work on time and the window for submission on MinerWriter has closed. After testing various solutions, we are currently allowing the individual instructor to decide whether or not the project should be evaluated. This helps us to ensure that students with legitimate reasons for not submitting on time are still able to receive credit.
13. Over the last five semesters, the committee has reviewed between six and ten grades a semester.

Works Cited

Beaufort, Anne. *College Writing and Beyond: A New Framework for University Writing Instruction*. Logan: Utah State UP, 2007. Print.

Broad, Bob, et al. *Organic Writing Assessment: Dynamic Criteria Mapping in Action*. Logan: Utah State UP, 2009. Print.

Centra, John A. *Reflective Faculty Evaluation: Enhancing Teaching and Determining Faculty Effectiveness*. San Francisco: Jossey-Bass, 1993. Print.

Chen, Yining, and Leon B. Hoshower. "Student Evaluation of Teaching Effectiveness: An Assessment of Student Perception and Motivation." *Assessment and Evaluation in Higher Education* 28.1 (2003): 71-88. Print.

Danielewicz, Jane, and Peter Elbow. "A Unilateral Grading Contract to Improve Learning and Teaching." *CCC* 61.2 (2009): 244-68. Print.

Gere, Anne Ruggles. "The Long Revolution in Composition." *Composition in the Twenty-First Century: Crisis and Change*. Ed. Lynn Z. Bloom, Donald A. Daiker, and Edward M. White. Carbondale: Southern Illinois UP, 1996. 119-32. Print.

Gouge, Catherine. "Conversation at a Crucial Moment: Hybrid Courses and the Future of Writing Programs." *College English* 71.4 (March 2009): 328-62. Print.

Grogan, Nedra, and Donald A. Daiker. "Team-Grading in College Composition." *WPA: Writing Program Administration* 13.1-2 (1989): 25-34. Print.

Haswell, Richard. *Beyond Outcomes: Assessment and Instruction in a University Writing Program*. Westport: Ablex, 2001. Print.

Herrington, Ann, Kevin Hodgson, and Charles Moran. "Technology, Change, and Assessment: What We Have Learned." *Teaching the New Writing: Technology, Change, and Assessment in the 21st-Century Classroom*. Ed. Ann Herrington, Kevin Hogdson, and Charles Moran. Berkeley: Teachers' College P, 2009. 198-208. Print.

Huot, Brian. *(Re)Articulating Writing Assessment for Teaching and Learning*. Logan: Utah State UP, 2002. Print.

Kemp, Fred. "Computers, Innovation, and Resistance in First-Year Composition Programs." *Discord and Direction: The Postmodern Writing Program Administrator*. Ed. Sharon James McGee and Carolyn Handa. Logan: Utah State UP, 2005. 105-22. Print.

---. Interview by Paula Wasley. "Freshman Comp, Revolutionized." *The Chronicle of Higher Education* 8 Mar. 2006: n.p. Web. 11 Nov. 2008.

Knievel, Michael. "Gauging the Value of Online Grade Posting: An Inquiry into Full Disclosure." *Kairos* 6.2 (2001): n.p. Web. 12 Nov. 2009.

Lang, Susan. "Comment and Response to 'Conversations at a Critical Moment: Hybrid Courses and the Future of Writing Programs.'" *College English* 72.5 (2010): 554-58. Print.

Peek, George S. "Grading by Jury: Accurate and Consistent." *Improving College and University Teaching* 30.2 (1982): 75-79. Print.

Penrod, Diane. *Composition in Convergence: The Impact of New Media on Writing Assessment*. Mahwah: Lawrence Erlbaum Associates, 2005. Print.

Rickly, Rebecca. "Distributed Teaching, Distributed Learning: Integrating Technology and Criteria-Driven Assessment into the Delivery of First-year Composition." *Delivering College Composition: The Fifth Canon*. Ed. Kathleen Blake Yancey. Portsmouth: Boynton/Cook, 2006. 183-98. Print.

Rojstaczer, Stuart, and Christopher Healey. "Grading in American Colleges and Universities." *Teacher's College Record*. Teacher's College, 4 Mar. 2010. Web. 12 Nov. 2009.

Schiming, Richard. "Grade Inflation Article." *Center for Excellence in Teaching and Learning*. Minnesota State U, n.d. Web. 12 Nov. 2009.

Sommers, Nancy. "Responding to Student Writing." *CCC* 33.2 (1982): 148-56. Print.

Sperling, Melanie. "Constructing the Perspective of Teacher-as-Reader: A Framework for Studying Response to Student Writing." *Research in the Teaching of English* 28.2 (1994): 175-207. Print.

Treglia, Maria O. "Teacher-Written Commentary in College Writing Composition: How Does It Impact Students' Revisions?" *Composition Studies* 37.1 (2009): 67-86. Print.

Wasley, Paula. "A New Way to Grade." *The Chronicle of Higher Education* 10 Mar. 2006: A6. Print.

White, Edward M. "Holistic Scoring: Past Triumphs, Future Challenges." *Validating Holistic Scoring for Writing Assessment: Theoretical and Empirical Foundations*. Ed. Michael M. Williamson and Brian A. Huot. Cresskill: Hampton P, 1993. 79-108. Print.

Whithaus, Carl. *Teaching and Evaluating Writing in the Age of Computers and High-stakes Testing*. Mahwah: Lawrence Erlbaum Associates, 2005. Print.

Yancey, Kathleen Blake. "Delivering College Composition into the Future." *Delivering College Composition: The Fifth Canon*. Ed. Kathleen Blake Yancey. Portsmouth: Boynton/Cook, 2006. 199-209. Print.

---. "Looking Back as We Look Forward: Historicizing Writing Assessment as a Rhetorical Act." *CCC* 50.3 (1999): 483-503. Print.

---. "Made Not Only in Words: Composition in a New Key." *CCC* 56.2 (2004): 297-328. Print.

Yancey, Kathleen Blake, Michael Bernard-Donals, Margaret Daisley, Maureen Neal, Steven VanderStaay, Nick Carbone and Brian Huot. "The Conversation Continues: A Dialogue on Grade Inflation." *The Theory and Practice of Grading Writing: Problems and Possibilities*. Ed. Frances Zak and Christopher Weaver. Albany: SUNY P, 1998. 185-92. Print.

What's in a Coauthor?: (Re)Locating Joseph Denney in Composition History

Ivan Davis

This article reassesses the Fred Newton Scott and Joseph Villiers Denney collaborative textbook authorship by emphasizing Denney's generally overlooked contributions to that coauthorship and to the field of composition generally. Through an examination of Denney's scholarly work and his personal correspondence with Scott during the period marking their collaborative textbook writing, this article asserts that Denney, like Scott, was an innovative theorist and practitioner in his own right, and that the effectiveness of the Scott-Denney textbooks owes much to Denney's role as coauthor.

Most of Fred Newton Scott's important textbooks were the result of collaborations, and arguably Scott's most important collaborator was Joseph Villiers Denney. Scott and Denney collaborated on four significant textbooks on English, including *Paragraph Writing* (1893), *Composition-Rhetoric* (1897), *Elementary English Composition* (1900), and *Composition-Literature* (1902). Albert R. Kitzhaber, James Berlin, Donald C. and Patricia L. Stewart, Robert J. Connors and others have acknowledged the distinctiveness of Scott and Denney's textbooks, particularly as they provide a less mechanistic approach to writing instruction than the work of their competitors. Nearly all such discussions of Scott and Denney's textbooks emerge from attempts to illuminate Scott's contributions to composition and rhetorical theory, while Denney's contributions and involvement are at best secondary considerations.

The regrettable implication in these discussions is that Denney was not a dynamic, equal partner in his collaborations with Scott, that Denney did not bring particular insights, interests and expertise to their textbook production or that these contributions cannot be distinguished from Scott's. Over time, this view has coalesced into something Lisa Mastrangelo has recently termed the discipline's "grand narrative" of Scott, an appreciation of Scott as a singular hero, which regrettably overlooks the fact that he was "part of the larger, organic movement in education, a networked group of teachers and scholars with shared goals and teaching practices" (251). As a result, this "grand narrative" conspires to make Denney a minor character in the story, if you will, effectively discounting his substantial work in the discipline of English and in higher education generally, while all but ignoring his writing on rhetoric and composition pedagogy. The conventional view also ignores

Scott's own estimation of Denney, for unquestionably, Scott had the highest regard for Denney, his longtime collaborator, colleague, and friend.

This article attempts a reassessment of the Scott-Denney collaboration by highlighting Denney's contributions to the partnership. Denney's role in the development of the coauthored textbooks and his treatment of composition pedagogy will be emphasized through an examination of his letters to Scott, which reveal the extent to which the two men collaborated in their textbook writing, and through an investigation of three significant articles on composition instruction that Denney wrote during the 1890s, the same period that saw the very productive Scott-Denney partnership begin. These articles are suggestive of Denney's particular interests in writing instruction. Among them, we find Denney emphasizing the relationship between reading and writing, particularly through the use of models for student writers, the fundamental importance of actual practice as the centerpiece of the composition class, and the instructional necessity of creating meaningful writing experiences for students. The articles prompt a reconsideration of the Scott-Denney textbook collaboration as they demonstrate the extent to which Denney's influence and thinking pervade those works.

Perhaps most intriguing, given Scott's reputation as a practitioner, is the extent to which Denney's expertise repeatedly targets the realm of classroom pedagogy or instructional methods. Throughout Denney's scholarly writing, we find him dealing with the practical concerns of the writing class in his attempt to produce a "systematic methodology" ("College Rhetoric" 39). His work in composition attempts to provide that framework, a three-part approach integrating the use of models for writing, actual practice in composing, and regular instructor feedback (40). This reassessment of Denney's contributions to the field concludes with a brief discussion of the least known Scott-Denney collaboration, *Aphorisms for Writing Teachers*, a short book distilling the fundamental tenets of their approach to teaching writing. Again, Denney's practical influence and contribution to the Scott-Denney collaboration can be seen in its pages, particularly in the section entitled "The Class Hour in English Composition."

Casting His Own Shadow

Both Scott's and Denney's roots were well established in the Midwest, roots that would only deepen during their long careers at the University of Michigan and the Ohio State University respectively.[1] The two men likely met while pursuing undergraduate degrees in English at the University of Michigan in 1881; Denney graduated one year after Scott in 1885 ("Denney" 285).[2] The two served as colleagues in the English department there during the 1890-91 school year, when Denney taught as an instructor while taking graduate courses (285). Scott, having been appointed as a faculty member only one year earlier, must have received Denney's arrival as a co-worker in the department with real enthusiasm.

However, Denney left the University of Michigan following the 1890-91 school year, not having completed the requirements for his master's degree (he was later awarded an honorary master's and an honorary doctorate degree), and, in 1891, began his long and distinguished career at Ohio State (285).

Probably more than his lack of earned advanced degrees, Denney's forays into administrative work at Ohio State—where notably he served as Dean of the College of Arts and in various other posts in addition to those in the English department—may have helped to diminish the perception of his role in coauthorship with Scott. As one of Denney's famous students, author and humorist James Thurber, notes, Denney "took on almost every administrative job in the university, ... [including] Acting President, Chairman of the Entrance Board, Secretary of the Faculty, and Director of the Summer Session" (202). While these duties doubtlessly contributed to Denney's reputation at Ohio State, his administrative work and increasing renown as a Shakespeare scholar, which Thurber also notes (204), may have increasingly overshadowed his research on composition and awareness of his textbook coauthorship with Scott. Additionally, Denney increasingly pursued other publication interests: textbooks on speech and debate, English programs at the elementary and high school levels, grammar instruction, as well as a number of edited collections of famous speeches and speakers.

However, Denney's legacy as an educator continues to be shaped primarily through his relationship to Scott via their coauthored textbooks on English.[3] Although generally regarded as inventive and unconventional, there is an underlying disappointment in the inability of the Scott-Denney textbooks to embody Scott's richest theoretical ideas on rhetoric and composition. Denney's scholarly work in composition mostly overlooked, his enduring reputation rests on this somewhat mixed appreciation for the Scott-Denney textbooks. On the one hand, it is the association and the work he is known for; on the other, because the textbooks are perhaps the least regarded in the Scott corpus, Denney's overall contribution to the field is diminished.

Though widely seen as the most innovative textbook, *Paragraph Writing*, for example, has been criticized for lacking "originality" and for being derivative of Genung and Bain (Stewart and Stewart 41; Kitzhaber 162). Similarly, *Composition-Rhetoric* has been called "mechanical" (Berlin, *Writing Instruction* 84), *Elementary English Composition* is criticized for devoting "two-thirds of its content to the four modes" (82), and *Composition-Literature* has been largely ignored or dismissed as "an anthology" rather than "a rhetoric" (Kitzhaber 218).

While praise for their textbook collaborations is tempered by this sort of criticism—that Scott and Denney should have gone further in implementing more of their advanced theoretical ideas—these same historians maintain that the textbooks stand out from other offerings of the time period. In assessing the impact of Scott and Denney's textbooks, Kitzhaber notes their influence on composition instruction, believing they helped to direct "the reform movement of the nineties" (71). Likewise, Berlin says the textbooks were able to offset the effects of "current-traditional" ideas by focusing "on the rhetorical context, a context that is always social and transactional in nature" (*Rhetoric* 49). These estimates suggest that Scott and Denney's textbooks initiated an alternative route to composition instruction at the time, affording teachers strategies to make learning to write an engaging and relevant endeavor. With their emphasis on student interests and knowledge, the social context of writing, and an approach to form grounded in psychology, Scott and Denney's textbooks were also popular because they were practical-minded. And perhaps that practical-mindedness determined the extent to which their more radical ideas could be included.

For various reasons, from publisher consideration of the marketplace to the belief that practicing teachers would find such textbooks too esoteric, scholars have tried to reconcile their disappointment in the textbooks with their high estimation of Scott's own scholarship. Again, by implication, this somewhat negative assessment of Scott and Denney's partnership contributes to diminishing Denney's relevance and reputation today. Taken further, these negative appraisals might also call into question Scott's decision to collaborate with Denney in the first place. The implications are unfortunate, for as we shall see, Denney was no tag-along in their coauthorship, nor was he unable to offer innovative and progressive thinking on composition instruction himself.

Navigating Coauthor(Ship)

A review of Denney's correspondence with Scott on the development of their textbooks illustrates the fully collaborative nature of their writing and rewriting process. The letters which specifically reference the production of revised editions of their popular textbooks often show Denney as the catalyst: dividing up responsibilities, suggesting ideas concerning form or subject matter, and initiating possible alterations.[4] In one dated September 12, 1907, Denney recounts for Scott the expectations of their publisher Mr. Allyn (of Allyn and Bacon) that new editions of *Elementary English Composition* and *Paragraph Writing* be completed. Denney himself promises Scott "a formidable list of suggestions" for revising *Elementary English Composition* and believes that for *Paragraph Writing*, "we should make a new book throughout." A subsequent letter from January 10, 1910, shows Denney again instigating revision plans. After noting the publisher's request that *Composition-Literature* be revised, Denney asks Scott, "Shall I tackle the job and also make a teachers' manual as I go along, submitting the result piece-meal to you with large, yawning gaps at various places, to be filled by you?" Further, Denney charts the course for the new edition, observing that there are "a good many chances for improvement, none, however, involving radical changes in the text." Even concerning issues nonessential to textbook content, Denney is not above prompting the course of action. In the same letter, Denney mentions the pressing deadline publishers are asking them to meet for the reprinting of *Composition-Literature*, and offers the hope that he and Scott might push the deadline back "a few weeks if we promised a revision and a manual."

Other comments from Denney indicate the extent to which he and Scott shared the responsibilities of textbook writing. Their authorship followed a standard pattern. Initially, Denney and Scott appear to have divided the textbook chores into large sections that each would be responsible for. Although this division of duties meant that they each wrote independently, the two carefully read each other's work, making suggestions for the other to consider while preparing the contribution for publication. Denney's comments in a letter dated February 17, 1908, illustrate how he and Scott coordinated their efforts. Denney tells Scott, "as to *P-W* [*Paragraph Writing*] I will try to close up my work on it before leaving here and will send it on to you with such suggestions as I have at hand for your part of it as soon as it is ready." Denney's work, it would appear, involved revamping the first half of *Paragraph Writing* for its reprinting, while the last half was Scott's responsibility. Later that same year, Denney writes to Scott that "it might be well for you to send me the copy for the last half of [*Paragraph Writing*] before you leave, so that I shall not repeat, in what I say in the first half" (Denney to Scott, May 28, 1908). In another example of their collaboration process, Denney discusses the revision of *Elementary English Composition* in a letter on June 30, 1915. After describing his own progress, Denney tells Scott, "Let me hear from you if you have any suggestions for the revision. My idea is not to alter much of the book after the first fifty pages." On another occasion, Denney tries to save Scott from additional obligations with their publishers. Denney tells Scott that the publishing company is demanding a teacher's manual for *Composition-Literature* and that he "will agree to do this for them, if ... [Scott] will sign in blank anything that I may say in the manual" (Denney to Scott, May 28, 1908). This sort of give-and-take between the two men, presumably prompted by Denney as often as by Scott, seems to be entirely ordinary when it comes to their textbook production.

As productive and cooperative as their professional relationship was, Scott and Denney were equally close on a personal level, a fact that plays out repeatedly in Denney's letters to Scott. There is little question that each man held the other in high esteem. Their Midwestern backgrounds, shared experiences at the University of Michigan, intellectual pursuits, and professional activities all contributed to this friendship. Similarly, their academic and professional alliances against the eastern schools' approaches to uniform reading lists, among other things, and, to a lesser degree, the demands of their publishers, must have strengthened their mutual bond.

Not surprisingly, then, Denney's letters digress into good-natured banter directed at his coauthor. In a letter from February 23, 1910, Denney writes Scott indicating that their publisher needs to know the sources for two quotations contained in *Composition-Literature*, and that Denney has been "baffled" in his attempts to locate them. Recognizing a mischievous impulse in Scott,

Denney slyly tells his collaborator, "I am compelled to believe that you wrote these yourself, expecting them to be attributed to Oliver Wendell Holmes or to Edward Everett Hale; but I will not ask you to confess it, if you will send on plausible references" to the publisher. In another instance, Denney equates his relationship to Scott with that portrayed in the "Alphonse and Gaston" comic strip, whose main characters continually and politely defer to one another.[5] He tells Scott, "we are both perfect in persuasion or else rivals of Alphonse and Gaston in the determination to yield to one another ... but should you decide otherwise I will not be slow to change my otherwise inflexible determination. [signed] Gaston" (Letter to Scott, June 3, 1919).

A Disciplinary Center—Composition

As in his letters to Scott, Denney's writing on rhetoric and composition during the 1890s, the same period during which he and Scott were conceiving the material for their textbooks, suggests he was a capable and productive collaborator. Like Scott, Denney is not only interested in the state of composition instruction in the colleges, but also instruction at the elementary and secondary levels. Among the topics he treats, Denney addresses the relationship between reading and composition, the effects of uniform reading lists on the English curriculum in the schools, the design of effective topics and assignments for student composition, and the necessary components of college writing instruction. It may be surprising to discover that Denney treats all of these vital and yet problematic areas within composition, but Denney, like Scott, also has the ability to make astute observations about then-current teaching practices, while offering theoretically-sound strategies for their improvement.

Frequently, however, Denney's writing on composition turns to the very practical concerns of classroom instruction. This is particularly interesting to note, as Scott typically has been regarded as the innovative practitioner. Yet a compelling picture develops from Denney's work, suggesting he played a major role in the formulation of the composition pedagogy that the Scott-Denney collaboration produced. Evidence from his articles combined with his probable authorship of the "The Class Hour" section in *Aphorisms* indicate that Denney's special interest and his contribution to their partnership came through this emphasis on practical classroom methods and concerns. It appears to have been his focus early on.

Writing in 1894, Denney bemoans the lack of a "systematic methodology" for teachers of writing, noting that "[i]t has been so much easier to compound a little psychology, logic, and philology, and to prescribe this compound under the name of Rhetoric, than to teach how to write, with all the drudgery of essay-correcting that is implied" ("College Rhetoric" 39). In contrast, Denney's own work posits an approach that views writing as an art. Were this view kept in mind, Denney argues, "how much text-book work, how much dawdling with manufactured errors, how much theoretical vaporing would disappear!" (39).

Building on this teaching-an-art vision of writing instruction, Denney advocates a threefold approach to classroom activities, including: "the study of models, practice in composing, and helpful criticism" (40). This paradigm predicts "clearly how the limited time usually allotted to Rhetoric in the college course should be occupied" (40). And it is through these touchstones—writing models, actual practice and teacher response—that Denney's theorizing on composition instruction, as well as his contributions to the Scott-Denney textbooks, can best be understood.

The implications of Denney's methods for writing instruction are perhaps more far-reaching than what one might expect. Throughout, his general procedure is to integrate—to incorporate literature with composition, to use oral exercises to facilitate composing, and to draw attention to meaning when addressing grammar and correctness in writing. As a result, the generic writing class one might associate with Denney's approach—and I think even the coursework Denney describes under the rubric "college rhetoric" would demonstrate this—emphasizes composition as an important means of developing better readers and users of language. Both implicitly and explicitly then, Denney argues that composition should play a central and unifying role in all English studies, promoting and integrating reading, grammar, literary study, rhetoric, and speech . His advocating of these connections in English education further demonstrates Denney's innovative theoretical and practical awareness, and provides additional evidence for his contribution to the Scott-Denney collaboration.

Perhaps the most consistent theme in Denney's work is the importance he places on reading and the use of models in writing instruction. Generally, Denney describes reading as functioning in two ways in the writing classroom: to broaden students' intellectual perspectives and to facilitate rhetorical analysis. And though an emphasis on models is featured in his work, Denney is adamant that reading play a secondary role to actual production in the writing classroom: "Neither interpretative reading nor any other kind of reading can take the place of practice in writing, for writing requires the exercise of certain powers which reading does not effectively compel to action when action is demanded of them" ("Two Problems" 4).

Denney advocates a familiar liberal arts orientation for the use of reading in the writing and English classroom. Reading the classics, according to Denney, can provide the benefit of "enlarging the sympathies, widening the intellectual horizon, and informing the spirit" (3). As a result, one of his goals when considering models in the writing class is for the instructor to emphasize "the thought and meaning to be found in them" ("English Requirements" 342). Reading also serves a second function in Denney's writing classroom, as the material and substance for guided rhetorical analysis, which has more "modest aims" and yet significantly "contributes directly to power in composition" ("Two Problems" 3). Rhetorical analysis in Denney's plan "points out the relations of part to part, it detects the literary expedients and devices that are common property. ... [and is] an aid in teaching how the difficulties of writing have been met and overcome" (3). And while this use of models for rhetorical analysis is more immediately practical for writing instruction than for the broadening of students' intellectual horizons, Denney indicates that its benefits "would not pay unless accompanied by [writing] practice at every step" (3).

Even when Denney's focus turns more exclusively to the study of literature and reading instruction, he includes a prominent place for writing. In his paper "English Requirements," which was shared at the meeting of the North Central Association of Colleges and Preparatory Schools in 1898 (later published in the *School Review*), Denney proposes a revamped approach to uniform reading lists for college admissions. Denney argues that secondary schools ought to reassess the way they meet these requirements, replacing the concentrated study of literature, a "minute and fidgety work" that "kills interest in the subject-matter" according to Denney (341), with instruction that would situate composition practice at the center of the English program.

> Put the work of the minimum requirement on the composition basis. ... [L]et all of the reading be utilized in daily composition work, oral and written, in reproduction of the reading, and on themes suggested by the reading, based on the observations and experience of the pupil. In this way we shall secure what is most needed in the schools: practice in writing, talking, and reading aloud. (341)

Denney's apparently radical proposal places "proficiency in composition" as the main objective, while still providing students the opportunity to cover the uniform reading requirements (342). Most significantly, Denney believes this realignment of composition and literary study could serve a vital role in helping students become more engaged readers with wider reading interests.

On still another level, Denney's ideas reflect a fairly modern understanding of the similarities and differences between the activities of reading and writing. For Denney, both reading and writing involve the activities of "abstraction," "selection," and "imagination" ("Two Problems" 5). In this respect, Denney's ideas point to our contemporary notion regarding the active role readers play as they engage texts—a foreshadowing of the work of Louise Rosenblatt and others who would highlight the transactional nature of reading. But Denney is also clear about the differences between writing and reading, and why reading must not supplant actual writing practice as the primary activity in the writing classroom.

> The application of selection, abstraction and imagination to elements already selected, abstracted and imagined by another is a very different thing from their application to a subject, thought, or set of circumstances which must be confronted for the first time. The reproductive process falls short of the creative process. (5)

The second of Denny's three pillars for classroom activities, actual practice in composing, is centered on the idea of providing meaningful writing assignments for students. Denney argues that only through meaningful writing—assignments that draw on students' individual observations and experiences—can composition instruction help students realize the full power of writing:

> The power to organize his own ideas, in written or oral speech, the power to deal with situations of which he is himself a vital part,—this is the power which composition-training seeks to develop in the pupil, and which practice in writing and speaking on subjects within the range of his own observation and experience can alone adequately call into activity. (5)

Initially, actual practice should focus on the level of the paragraph—the discourse unit of choice for Denney and Scott (a fact highlighted by their most popular textbook, *Paragraph Writing*). Yet at any level of discourse, whether a sentence or complete essay, Denney believes that the thought of the student, and the clear expression of that thought, should be the foremost concern.

Denney's primary method for making writing meaningful for students is through writing assignment design, a topic he takes up in "Two Problems in Composition-Teaching." In the article, Denney provides some clear principles about how teachers of writing should design topics for student writing assignments. Denney proposes that topics be drawn from student interests and connected with observations and experiences in their lives. In fact, one of the striking features of Denney and Scott's textbooks is their insistence on these same sorts of topics for writing. First, Denney asserts that essay topics must prompt "real life" situations, where the subject matter "suggest[s] a personal relationship to the situation" for the writer, and "a particular reader or set of readers" to be addressed (7). One of the best ways of proceeding, according to Denney, is by formulating topics that "suggest a problem for solution," because these sorts of assignments require "all of the resources of the pupil" (7).

As examples, Denney cites vague writing prompts like "a description of this city," "foreign missions," and "bee-keeping" (7), noting that each does little in shaping a sense of audience or purpose for student writers. Denney revises each to emphasize rhetorical constraints that can generate something closer to "real life" communication (7). For the city description, Denney asks students to compose "a description of this city written by a property-owner to induce a retired farmer to take up his abode among us, with some account of our superior educational advantages" (7). "Foreign missions" becomes "an attempt to induce a business man who has never given foreign missions any consideration, to contribute to their support," and "bee-keeping" is revamped to "would bee-keeping be profitable to the farmers of this county?—written for the Farmer's Institute by a student of the Agricultural College" (7). At stake in such topic design is the heightening of the social context of writing and communicating. Topics must "present a real social situation to be attacked," because these will offer the student the best preparation for "what he will have to do every day of his life in his dealing with men" (7-8). This is a highly pragmatic goal, and suggests that Denney sees all instruction in composition leading toward the effective communication of thought, not the mere exercise of correctness in grammatical form or generic structure.

It seems Denney felt strongly that, for beginning writers, composing at the level of the paragraph provides the best opportunity for immediate practice and growth. In fact, paragraph instruction is at the heart of the first term writing course Denney describes in his article "College Rhetoric." Like the position he and Scott take in *Paragraph Writing,* the theoretical justification for teaching the paragraph at this stage is compelling, as Denney believes the paragraph is a "miniature essay," which, because it is longer than the sentence, allows instructors to focus on expressive modes ("College Rhetoric" 43). Such "tools of expression" that include "comparison and analogy," "contrast and negation," "repetition" and other types Denney mentions can all be practiced effectively in composing paragraphs (44-5). Through practice and study, the student comes to see the value of these tools, particularly, and importantly, when "it is one of his own ideas that is calling for development" (44) through these tools. Denney also notes how careful study of the paragraph and practice in paragraph composition teach students more traditional rhetorical concepts. This focus on the paragraph, according to Denney, illustrates "in concrete form the general laws of composition—unity, selection, proportion, sequence, and variety" (46).

From paragraph instruction, Denney envisions a relatively uncomplicated shift to full essay writing within the first-year course. In fact, teaching the paragraph enables students to see "the pleasing functional analogy that exists between sentences in the paragraph and paragraphs in the essay" (46). Expressive modes evolve in similar fashions in both the paragraph and essay, with the only new aspects being "the forming of transitions, introductions, conclusions, the application of the laws of association to the order of topics in the outline, and the consideration of proportion of parts" (47). It is the focus on the essay that completes the first-year writing course, which Denney calls "Practical Rhetoric," because of its emphasis on practice in "writing, personal consultation [with the instructor], revising, and re-writing—all with a view to clear thinking and clear expression" (47).

Moving beyond the paragraph and the first term course, Denney's approach to advanced work in writing at the university level reiterates his desire to create meaningful writing experiences for students. In the advanced course, Denney proposes a more sophisticated and yet highly practical orientation for writing instruction that would reflect the student's major area or professional goals. "The ideal," Denney says, "would be individual instruction having reference to individual needs, tastes, lines of work, and purposes" (48). Denney separates the program into two large divisions: the academic course and the technical course. Students in the academic course receive more traditional rhetorical training, including "studies in style," "investigation of technical questions in style," "principles of criticism," and "the development of rhetorical theory" (48-9). Rhetorical analysis becomes a major part of the academic course, as students produce numerous reports examining various writers and models.

Denney's technical course, however, is more forward-thinking, and undoubtedly reflects his experience with Ohio State students who were studying in the agriculture department and brought with them varying backgrounds and professional goals. For models, Denney envisions writing instructors making use of various professional journals and magazines as practical and realistic examples of style. As part of actual practice, writing tasks in the technical course include magazine articles, memoranda, laboratory reports, "brief-making," "story-writing, newspaper forms and correspondence" (51). Denney is insistent about the reasons that should prompt student production, not only in the technical course, but throughout the writing curriculum. Denney cautions that "in these as in the earlier courses the idea of writing with a purpose and an occasion in view is kept prominent" (51). A recurring theme in his and Scott's work is the belief that when composition is "connected with reality at every step, the study can not fail to be of great value" (52).

Perhaps surprisingly, Denney says the least about "helpful criticism," third in his pedagogical framework, although one certainly recognizes the program he has in mind when he uses the term. Importantly, instructor feedback comes within the context of the first of Denney's three-part approach to the writing classroom: the rhetorical analysis of models. So part of "helpful criticism" begins with the instructor's role in leading students through an examination of writing models. Left at that, however, such analysis might be limited to merely "detect[ing] and nam[ing] figures of speech" (43).

What Denney means by "helpful criticism," however, proposes that instructors utilize analysis so as to produce an understanding of students' work within the rhetorical constraints of subject matter, form, audience, etc. One senses that Denney's "helpful criticism" consists primarily of turning the teacher's rhetorical analysis toward the work of his or her students in an attempt to improve their writing. Additionally, Denney's reliance on speaking, talking and formal activities like "oral composition" in the writing classroom suggests that students can provide each other with at least some limited version of this "helpful criticism" focusing on rhetorical issues ("Two Problems" 6). The teacher and other students are involved. Primarily, however, Denney's concept of criticism involves instructor feedback and guidance within the process of students writing. In full, such criticism, "under wise and inspiring direction," aims "to help ... pupils to a better self-expression" (6). And it is an approach that Denney believes should go beyond the writing classroom to be "part of the business of every teacher, whatever his subject" (6).

Still further, and building on Denney's notion of crafting meaningful, "real life" writing assignments, effective instructor feedback fosters more than just students' ability to "identify structural forms of good prose" (8). Through practice and criticism, students will "identify the structural forms selected as functions of the situation to be attacked," to see that the structure they use

> in a particular case must be used advisedly, its choice or rejection being determined by the function it is expected to fulfill. The grammatical, rhetorical, and logical forms of expression employed would thus demand, in any given case, their full explanation in the use to which they were to be put. (8)

Helpful instructor criticism, it would appear, functions in the writing class to demand that "full explanation" from students. And it is here that Denney ultimately locates a standard for instructor feedback and response:

> The minutest criticism made would find its sufficient reason in a better statement of the thought in view of the particular situation presented and the particular reader and writer designated; and even questions of punctuation would acquire importance as thought-questions, rather than as form questions. The whole system of criticism would become more helpful to the pupil because it would rest on a more reasonable foundation. (8)

"Chicken Soup" for Writing Instructors

Probably Scott and Denney's least known collaborative effort, *Aphorisms for Teachers of English Composition* (1905), provides the most revealing overview of their approach to teaching composition. Although not receiving much critical attention, *Aphorisms* has been called "one of the friendliest and most inspirational books" Scott ever wrote (Stewart and Stewart 73). Only twenty three pages, the book condenses Scott and Denney's fundamental beliefs concerning teachers, students, theory and practice in the teaching of composition. The book accomplishes this through its collage-like form; picture a book of proverbs, only loosely arranged around subheadings, written for composition instructors. These short passages, some only a sentence or two long, reveal highly concentrated ideas that have multiple levels of significance. *Aphorisms* illustrates how popular Scott and Denney's other textbooks had become by this time, as it likely filled a desire on the part of teachers to have further guidance from the two prominent textbook authors. Remarkably, and in spite of its small size, the book packs quite a punch.

The conception of composition instruction that evolves from a reading of *Aphorisms* is striking for a number of reasons, not the least of which is Scott and Denney's obvious conviction about composition's value and importance. In *Aphorisms*, Scott and Denney outline composition's practical value to the individual student and to society at large; they carefully examine the necessary qualifications and personal traits of the model composition teacher; they provide clear guidance for approaching students as developing humans who are capable of clear thinking and expression if given proper instruction; and they discuss classroom methods ranging from assignment design to in-class composing to peer review workshops. Indeed, through all that it covers, *Aphorisms* provides the most concise and yet comprehensive statement of Scott and Denney's beliefs about the entire project of teaching composition.

The content divisions in *Aphorisms* suggest an arrangement between Scott and Denney that is similar to the division of writing duties in their other textbooks. It appears that Denney was largely responsible for the final section, "The Class Hour in English Composition,"[6] and that Scott—and Denney, to a lesser extent—developed material for the preceding sections. "The Class Hour in English Composition" covers so many of the same concerns that Denney highlights in his own writing, that his influence on the section is unmistakable. Such items as writing with a purpose, prewriting and planning strategies, reading and analyzing models, teacher response, connections between speaking, reading, and writing, outlets for student publication—all of these items bear Denney's influence.[7] Although it is impossible to know definitively who wrote what, given the precedent set in earlier collaborations, there is little doubt that Scott and Denney shared the writing responsibilities of *Aphorisms* as well.

One of the most pronounced impressions that *Aphorisms* leaves is its focus on students' needs and abilities. Regularly drawing on disciplines outside of English to inform their teaching of writing, Scott and Denney's approach is often associated with advancements in psychology, particularly developmental psychology. But Scott and Denney describe the teacher's need for a psychological understanding of their students in much more personal tones. Teachers must have "a deeper knowledge of the capacity, tastes, and interests of the individual pupils. Psychology at large is interesting; but the psychology of young Tommy Smith, as discovered in his themes, is much more interesting" (8). In fact, "every interest which pupils can have, the teacher of composition must have also. He must be able to say truthfully: Nothing in student humanity do I consider foreign to myself" (8). For Scott and Denney, this knowledge of, and sensitivity to, student interests distinguishes the teacher of writing. In sum, the writing teacher's philosophy must be a "philosophy of adolescence" (9).

That approximately a third of *Aphorisms* is given over to teaching methods under the subheading, "The Class Hour in English Composition" (17-23), is perhaps unremarkable. In fact, it may have been the most anticipated portion of the booklet for readers interested in pragmatic concerns. The ultimate irony, however, is that Denney authors the very section of *Aphorisms* on which Scott's legacy is generally built: pedagogical innovation. Once more, the divisions of their shared authorship suggests the importance of Denney's contributions.

In "The Class Hour," we find Scott and Denney's pedagogical formula: writing is best learned through practice, and students must write with a sense of purpose, seek self-expression in their writing, and envision a particular reader or audience. Because Scott and Denney believe writing is an art, they insist that composition class time should "find the class in the practice of the art" (18). Further, class time must present students with "a sharply defined object, that the pupil may learn, whenever he writes, to write with a purpose in mind" (19). The teacher must coordinate practice and purpose through instructional methods. Scott and Denney summarize their approach this way:

> Though we are thinking all the time of the purpose and of the subject matter, we are also raising questions of art and are teaching the laws and principles of art,—unity, selection, proportion, variety, method, and the rest. These questions are more easily answered when a particular reader is named beforehand. (20)

Scott and Denney provide even more striking suggestions concerning the teacher's role in stimulating prewriting, in correcting themes, and in publishing student essays. *Aphorisms* includes a number of strategies for prewriting and invention. The authors suggest that "observation," "reading," and "note-taking" all play a role in preparation for writing, and that an entire class benefits from individual students sharing their ideas with the larger group (19). Similarly, *Aphorisms* champions the regular use of writing models in the writing course. With models, the authors maintain, mechanical issues such as sentence structure, precise phrasing, punctuation, "and the simpler procedures of rhetoric" can be taught effectively and provide students with options they can employ in their own writing (20-1). Scott and Denney also believe that speaking and speech-making should be given "a larger place" in the composition class, so that students may receive additional composing practice (21). In fact, Scott and Denney feel so strongly about actual writing practice being at the center of composition instruction that they say "the class hour should be occupied more than half the time in writing or in oral composition" (23). Each of these ideas, as we have seen, has been previously asserted by Denney in his own scholarship on composition, lending further credence to his influence here in "The Class Hour" section of *Aphorisms*.

In spite of its brief form, *Aphorisms* highlights many of Scott and Denney's concerns about composition instruction, and in doing so, demonstrates how they believe some of the more significant practical issues teachers and students face should be addressed. Their approach is a practical merger between student-centered and skill-centered pedagogies, where teachers attempt to connect and adapt increasingly mature concepts and ideas with students' curiosities, desires and capabilities—themes that have long been associated with Scott's work, and, should now be noted, evidenced in the work of his longtime collaborator as well.

Epilogue

As the decades passed, although Denney's career moved increasingly into literary study and administrative duties at the Ohio State University—as in fact Scott's career became similarly more concerned with journalism at the University of Michigan—there are indications of Denney's continued interest in composition. Notably, in 1918, Denney published "Preparation of College Teachers of English" in *English Journal*,[8] where he takes up the issue of preparing graduate students to teach introductory composition and literature courses, which then, as now, were typically geared to "freshman" undergraduate students. According to Denney, it is these courses that present a particular set of issues, problems that "older heads have failed thus far to solve" (326). In spite of his changing priorities and duties, and probably because of his role as chair of the English department at Ohio State, Denney had undoubtedly continued to consider the best methods for training instructors to implement the sort of pedagogical practices he and Scott had championed.

Denney's proposal for teacher training is a distinctly modern-sounding seminar course in teaching composition. Among those topics to be covered, Denney lists

> The specific aims of the elementary [freshman] courses; the necessity for such courses; the bearings of psychology on current practice; the proper content of such courses; the order of topics; the best basis of differentiating students into groups for instruction; the use of the conference period; co-operative schemes among departments; the grammar question; oral composition; [and] the measurement of results. (326)

Additionally as part of the program, Denney anticipates class "visitation" and "a little practice teaching," which would be overseen by "experienced members of the department" and include observations and "reports" that are assessed department-wide (326). Like the introduction to composition theory courses now found in most universities offering graduate degrees in English, Denney's model seeks to provide students with a broad initiation into the practices of teaching writing.

Here, as in his earlier scholarship and collaborative textbooks with Scott, Denney's conception brings together the practical and theoretical, and emphasizes the value that should be attached to composition instruction by recognizing that it is a vocation not only worthy of but necessitating rigorous preparation—an idea that was not terribly in vogue during the period in which he writes. Indeed, with the obvious exception of Denney's longtime collaborator at the University of Michigan, there seems to be little evidence of intentional and well-conceived programs for training teachers of composition at this time. Still, Denney's innovative approach to teacher preparation suggests we would continue to benefit by probing and questioning the discipline's "grand narrative" concerning the work and contributions of Fred Newton Scott.

Notes

1. While Scott had been born and raised in Indiana, Denney was born in Aurora, Illinois, in 1862, making him Scott's junior by less than a year-and-a-half. Whereas Scott's father was a judge and politician, Denney's father had been a

recent immigrant from England, making his living as a furniture manufacturer ("Denney" 285). Presumably, their Midwestern upbringings contributed to the mutual affection each had for the other.
2. Following graduation, and work as a newspaper reporter and editor, Denney taught at East High School in Aurora, Illinois, and served as principal there from 1888-1890 (Thurber 201; "Denney" 285).
3. This reputation also ignores other textbooks Denney wrote, coauthored and edited.
4. Although no comparable collection of letters from Scott to Denney is available to examine, we can assume that Scott's letters to Denney contained the same sort of directives. That their relationship allowed for this type of give-and-take is implied in Denney's letters to Scott.
5. "Alphonse and Gaston" was written and illustrated by Frederick Burr Opper. The strip satirically treated two overly polite Frenchmen.
6. In fact, the complete title of the booklet appears to be *Aphorisms for Teachers of English Composition and The Class Hour in English Composition*—perhaps further evidence of Scott and Denney's likely division of labor.
7. Sections in the first part of *Aphorisms*, particularly "Of Sympathy" and "Living to Teach," seem more in line with Scott's work, especially ideas he advanced in *The Teaching of English in the Elementary and the Secondary School* in 1903.
8. The article was originally presented in November of 1916 to the college section at the National Council of Teachers of English in New York.

Works Cited

Berlin, James. *Rhetoric and Reality: Writing Instruction in American Colleges, 1900-1985*. Carbondale: Southern Illinois UP, 1987. Print.

---. *Writing Instruction in Nineteenth-Century American Colleges*. Carbondale: Southern Illinois UP, 1984. Print.

Connors, Robert J. *Composition-Rhetoric: Backgrounds, Theory, and Pedagogy*. Pittsburgh: U of Pittsburgh P, 1997. Print.

Denney, Joseph V. "College Rhetoric." *Proceedings of the Annual Conventions of the Modern Language Association of Ohio* (1894-95): 39-52. Print.

---. "English Requirements." *School Review* 6 (1898): 339-43. Print.

---. Letter to Fred Newton Scott. 12 Sep. 1907. MS. Fred Newton Scott Papers. Bentley Historical Lib., Ann Arbor.

---. Letter to Fred Newton Scott. 17 Feb. 1908. MS. Fred Newton Scott Papers. Bentley Historical Lib., Ann Arbor.

---. Letter to Fred Newton Scott. 28 May 1908. MS. Fred Newton Scott Papers. Bentley Historical Lib., Ann Arbor.

---. Letter to Fred Newton Scott. 10 Jan. 1910. MS. Fred Newton Scott Papers. Bentley Historical Lib., Ann Arbor.

---. Letter to Fred Newton Scott. 23 Feb. 1910. MS. Fred Newton Scott Papers. Bentley Historical Lib., Ann Arbor.

---. Letter to Fred Newton Scott. 30 June 1915. MS. Fred Newton Scott Papers. Bentley Historical Lib., Ann Arbor.

---. Letter to Fred Newton Scott. 3 June 1919. MS. Fred Newton Scott Papers. Bentley Historical Lib., Ann Arbor. Print.

---. "Preparation of College Teachers of English." *English Journal* 7.5 (1918): 322-26. Print.

---. "Two Problems in Composition-Teaching." *Contributions to Rhetorical Theory 3*. Ed. Fred Newton Scott. Ann Arbor: Inland P, 1896. Print.

"Denney, Joseph Villiers." *The National Cyclopaedia of American Biography*. Vol. XLIV. New York: James T. White and Co., 1962. 285-6. Print.

Kitzhaber, Albert R. *Rhetoric in American Colleges, 1850-1900*. Dallas: Southern Methodist UP, 1990. Print.

Mastrangelo, Lisa. "Lone Wolf or Leader of the Pack?: Rethinking the Grand Narrative of Fred Newton Scott." *College English* 72.3 (2010): 248-68. Print.

Rosenblatt, Louise M. *The Reader the Text the Poem: The Transactional Theory of the Literary Work*. Carbondale: Southern Illinois UP, 1978. Print.

Scott, Fred Newton, George R. Carpenter, and Franklin T. Baker. *The Teaching of English in the Elementary and the Secondary School*. New York: Longmans, Green and Co., 1903. Print.

Scott, Fred Newton, and Joseph V. Denney. *Aphorisms for Teachers of English Composition*. Boston: Allyn and Bacon, 1905. Print.

---. *Composition-Literature*. Boston: Allyn and Bacon, 1902. Print.

---. *Composition-Rhetoric*. Boston: Allyn and Bacon, 1897. Print.

---. *Elementary English Composition*. Boston: Allyn and Bacon, 1900. Print.

---. *Paragraph Writing*. Boston: Allyn and Bacon, 1893. Print.

Stewart, Donald C., and Patricia L. Stewart. *The Life and Legacy of Fred Newton Scott*. Pittsburgh: U of Pittsburgh P, 1997. Print.

Thurber, James. *The Thurber Album*. New York: Simon and Schuster, 1952. Print.

Course Design

Teaching as Text—The Pedagogy Seminar: LIT 730, Teaching Composition

Janet Auten

Course Description

LIT 730: Teaching Composition is a three-credit graduate seminar in American University's Department of Literature for master's-degree students interested in teaching composition. The Literature Department offers both an MA in Literature and an MFA in Creative Writing, and attracts applicants with a flexible "teaching concentration" option as part of their four-semester MA and five-semester MFA course work. The seminar functions as both a course in Composition Studies and an introduction to pedagogy for fifteen graduate students each fall.

Institutional Context

American University (AU) is a private, four-year, research-oriented institution located in a leafy northwest residential section of Washington, DC. Many of its 6800 undergraduate students come to the university for its location in the nation's capital, but virtually all of them must complete a two-course sequence of first-year composition (FYC) in the department's College Writing Program. With fifty-three master's and ten doctoral programs, American University also serves about 3600 grad students, with an additional 1700 students in its nationally-prominent law school. The Department of Literature has no PhD program and attracts grad students who either plan to continue on into doctoral studies elsewhere or hope to support themselves by teaching in high school or community college.

For such a department, with no PhD or rhetoric/composition program, neither a TA-training class nor a full-blown composition theory course makes sense. LIT 730, like most such "orientation" courses, is not part of a series that gradually deepens students' exposure to the field but rather is a singular course that seeks to ground future practice in theory and provide an intellectual foundation for teaching. It combines a theory-oriented Composition Studies course and a practice-focused Teaching Writing course for graduate students who want to acquire knowledge that can be translated into marketable job skills. After LIT 730, they may gain practical experience in the department as literature class TAs, College Writing classroom interns working with a writing faculty mentor, or Writing Center interns working with students one-to-one. So, unlike the literature department's other courses in subject and purpose, LIT 730 operates in an adjunct intellectual space all its own. Fittingly, perhaps, I have taught it for ten years as adjunct faculty (in addition to my duties as full-time director of the Writing Center).

When I took on the moribund Teaching of Writing seminar in Fall, 2000, I maintained the standard survey-course approach that my predecessor had set up and turned to my own graduate school staples: Edward P. J. Corbett, Nancy Myers, and Gary Tate's *Writing Teacher's Sourcebook* and Erika Lindemann's classic, comprehensive *A Rhetoric for Writing Teachers*. But unlike my graduate school pedagogy course, LIT 730 is a stand-alone seminar, a one-shot survey that presents pressures for coverage. As Shelley Reid puts it, even as I stuffed the assignment list, "always there were more topics and tasks and articles, all waiting for me to cover them in my fifteen-week class" (15). And my frustration in trying to provide such "coverage" was matched by student frustration with the material. One student wrote in his end-of-semester reflection:[1] "Weekly, it seemed I was bombarded with weighty discussions of the history and theory of composition and I reached a low point several weeks into the semester when I was forced to acknowledge in a journal entry that I had no idea what the readings were trying to say." My initial impulse to douse students in reading gave way as I realized how these MA and MFA candidates, though eager to teach, were frustrated "when faced with significant, challenging reading and writing assignments grounded in an unfamiliar field of study often devalued in part because of its association with pedagogy" (Belanger and Gruber 123).

My students love writing, but many are brought up short at the entrance to Composition Studies by the different demands of its important texts. They must navigate readings grounded in social science, from the cognitive theory of Flower and Hayes to contemporary studies of composing on computers. Some simply balk at scholarly prose. Douglas Hesse captures their initial attitude with almost comical accuracy: "'Why can't these people write?' they challenge ... [S]tudents resisted material that was new to them ... comparing these readings to texts as they imagined texts should be" (225). Many of my students seemed to stay polite outsiders, visitors to the rhetoric/composition kingdom, just looking to pick up some new skills. I needed to bridge the divide between students in literary studies and Creative Writing and this foreign field of Composition Studies. Like Reid, I have come to see the pedagogy course "as practice in a way of encountering the world rather than mastery of skills or facts, as preparation for a lifetime of *thinking like a teacher*" (16).

Theoretical Rationale

I redesigned LIT 730 to lead students more explicitly toward thinking like teachers by helping them make connections between personal and academic experience, engaging them explicitly in theorizing, and making our classroom a kind of laboratory in which we interact and then reflect on our interactions. Paul Kameen talks about "the textuality of the classroom and what we do there ... as eligible for, even demanding of, our most careful, sophisticated, complex, critical scrutiny" (172). I present LIT 730 as such a text, not so much a template for "real world" teaching but a construct, a matter of *intentional artifice*: let's look at how I built this course; let's examine what we're doing, and, together, let's figure out why we're doing it.

With such meta-awareness in mind, I arrange the class to parallel the first-year writing course these graduate students are preparing to teach. Through class activities such as freewriting, small group work, and peer editing, the course demonstrates the pedagogical moves these that would-be teachers might make in their own classrooms. In assigning reading response papers and two academic essays, I guide students toward more awareness of their own academic writing while sensitizing them to the struggles of their students to learn "the moves," as Gerald Graff and Cathy Birkenstein call it, of a new discipline. To further this goal, I recently added Graff and Birkenstein's *They Say/I Say: The Moves that Matter in Academic Writing*, a book that our College Writing Program faculty frequently assign in their FYC courses. The slim Graff and Birkenstein textbook offers both a writer's guide to the "moves" of academic writing and a way of talking about how one teaches them in FYC. It is easy to forget that not all grad students have acquired skill in analyzing the "moves" academic authors make, much less the ability to bring that analysis to bear on what happens not only in their readings but also in a classroom.

My teaching of LIT 730 also has been influenced by compositionists' calls for a more reflective stance in teaching and the need for paying attention to the personal in our pedagogy. In *Seeing Yourself as a Teacher*, Elizabeth Rankin outlines some key factors that influenced the graduate students she interviewed as they struggled to assume teacher identities: personal history, theoretical orientation, and expectations about teaching. Building on feedback from students and on current scholarship, I developed LIT 730 to target the student-to-teacher transformation in three ways: by demystifying composition theory, by putting students in conversation with composition's key ideas, and by pointing them toward reflective practice.

From the outset, LIT 730 must make students aware of the need for a well-grounded, theorized practice, yet it must also help them realize that they "already have theories about teaching, rooted in contexts and experiences that may be obvious or long buried" (Reid 19). The first class opens by calling students' attention to pedagogy: without any introductions, I march into the room and briskly demand that they take out pen and paper and write an essay about their experience with academic writing. After allowing them five minutes of dutiful scribbling, I interrupt to question my own imperialist introduction—and their acquiescence to it. My questions—*How did you know what to do? Why did you automatically obey me?*—both relieve the tension my bit of acting created and lead to exploration of the academic context in which we learn and teach. Later in that first class, students share anecdotes about their own literacy education in small groups and discover common themes about how writing is taught in the academy. The combination of active theorizing and self-reflexive awareness addresses students' anxiety and even hostility to "theory," and I conclude the class by noting that they have been engaging in theory-making themselves.

The initial reading and response assignment, which deals with the theory and practice of teaching in the academy, is an invitation to enter a conversation in unfamiliar territory for most of these students: it introduces the discourse of Composition Studies with David Bartholomae's classic "Inventing the University" and Kathleen Blake Yancey's call to teach "Writing in the 21st Century" and raises the notion of merging the personal and the academic with Mike Rose's narrative essay, "I Just Wanna Be Average" from *Lives on the Boundary*. A chapter from Gerald Graff's *Clueless in Academe* both defines academic discourse and illustrates ways of theorizing teaching by combining analysis and anecdotes. The response paper prompt and, later, the first more formal paper assignment both ask students to use their own experiences in the academy in conjunction with their insights from the reading as a way of *examining* academic literacy. Rose's autobiographical essay offers a model to these budding fiction writers and literary scholars for taking academic literacy personally. An important task for the early writing assignments is to help students navigate between personal experience and scholarship, encouraging them to access the advantages of both as they discover that they complement rather than oppose each other. Like Bartholomae, I want students to find "some compromise between idiosyncrasy, a personal history, on the one hand, and the requirements of convention, the history of a discipline, on the other hand" (3) in their response papers and that first essay.

Meanwhile, the course structure leads us from acknowledging the personal and professional contexts of composition to examining its theoretical underpinnings. We look first at literacy itself, asking questions like "what difference does writing make?" with selections from the classic—Plato's *Phaedrus*—and contemporary—a chapter from Naomi Baron's 2008 *Always On: Language in an Online and Mobile World*. Next, we consider the composing process with Sondra Perl, Rose's discussion of writer's block ("Rigid Rules"), and a recent piece from *RTE* in which Anish Dave and David Russell discuss how composing on the computer has changed the nature of students' composing habits. With an eye for intersections between their reading and their lived experience, students complete a questionnaire about their own writing habits before composing their response papers about their reading on composing. In her end-of-semester evaluation, one student concluded that this structure "provided me with a deeper understanding of classroom dynamics, the process of writing, and ideas for structuring my own classroom … [and] my consciousness of my own writing process lends insight into what I must teach."

The next few weeks of the course are devoted to particular stages in teaching the writing process: invention (Elbow's "Closing My Eyes as I Speak" and Ann Berthoff's discussion of generating chaos in "From *the Making of Meaning*" are both in our anthology) and revision (classic pieces from Joseph Harris and Nancy Sommers). I ask students to use the assigned

Harris and Sommers articles to help them revise and then write a reflective page or two on their revision process as they turn in their first major essay. The complexity of commenting and evaluation appear next, as part of our survey of the writing process, drawing attention to the *teacher's* process and the fact that evaluation is an inherent part of this academic writing context we're working in.

At the midpoint of the course comes debate night. After reading Berlin, Bartholomae, and Elbow, students must first take on what I call a "teacherly self," selecting one of the pedagogical approaches outlined by Berlin that seems to suit them best. Then they prepare for class by choosing a pedagogical stance that is *different* from one(s) they favor and outline arguments in favor of that stance. In class, they debate the merits of changing the direction of a fictitious university writing program, taking on the voices of faculty members and arguing for the approach to FYC that they didn't favor. Each year, this complex reverse structure causes me anxiety (*Will it work this time? Will they all choose the same side?*) but then evokes my relief and respect as students invariably rise to the occasion. After the debate itself, we discuss how such oppositional discourse not only supports critical thinking but also helps participants recognize the strengths in the opposing points of view. In the ten-minute writing time that closes the evening, students can capture emerging teaching philosophies as they write down the most important insights they gained from the debate and try to craft "5 solid sentences about teaching writing."

I take a Bakhtinian perspective on disciplinarity. I want students to view composition scholarship in terms of various voices engaged in conversation. The weekly reading assignments invite students to consider different angles on an issue. In-class activities such as the debate put students and scholarship in dialogue by "dramatizing the rhetorical space of the classroom so that the new teachers [will] think more carefully about their own positions as teacher-rhetors in the first-year writing classroom" (Stancliff and Goggin 15). Starting in the third week, pairs of students lead a 45-minute discussion on the week's reading. They are asked not only to sign up for the week of their choice but also to prepare a lesson plan for engaging texts and classmates in lively dialogue.

Similarly, in the second half of the semester, the burden of guiding/prompting weekly response essays shifts to students themselves. Each week, three or four students write and post prompts of their own for everyone to respond to online (we use a discussion board platform in Blackboard, but this can be done on a blog or in any online discussion space). The writer may not select his or her own prompt to write on. By putting students in charge of the response assignments, I cede more authority to them and also mandate a kind of peer-reviewed tryout in the key skill of crafting writing prompts. Students must find the middle ground between withholding their own interpretations, on the one hand, and leaving writers to flounder around in generalizations on the other. I remind them, too, how lost they felt that first day with only a peremptory command, "write an essay," to follow. So this assignment to create assignments puts students in dialogue with me—representing the profession—as well as with each other, now representing both teaching colleagues and future students.

Later in the semester, I highlight the sense of professional dialogue with a panel/roundtable discussion featuring some department composition professionals: full-time faculty in the College Writing Program. It is sometimes a challenge to convince graduate students of the practicality in professional conversations about composition. Over the years, I have tried in various ways to inject the "real-world' element into the course: sometimes requiring students to visit one or two college writing classes, some years scheduling serial visits from individual writing faculty to talk about classroom practice, but the panel/roundtable format has proved especially popular and effective. I invite colleagues who represent an array of teaching approaches and backgrounds to come to our class prepared to discuss the week's reading assignments and their own practice with us. The faculty talk about their course syllabi, offer opinions in discussing the reading, and share anecdotes in response to students' questions about "what happens when…" in FYC classrooms. Class discussion after the faculty leave raises issues of institutional expectations and programmatic demands as a rhetorical problem: teaching FYC means meshing one's personal goals with those of the larger program.

Another way of drawing students into dialogue with the profession involves the other major writing assignment. This has taken a variety of forms over the years—book reviews, annotated bibliographies, reading reports—but it focuses invariably on recent publications in the field and urges students to become acquainted with professional journals while they pursue an interest in some specific teaching topic. I provide some focus in the form of quotations from composition scholars followed by broad prompts (e.g. "Which composition theorist do you think is most helpful and/or essential in preparing new teachers for a self-reflective practice?"). The assignment also requires students to make a lesson plan, create a handout, and "teach" a 15-minute segment of class, presenting their findings in an engaging way. Students have created lively mini-lessons using video, small-group work, and even role-playing.

The second half of the semester's reading turns to contemporary ideas on teaching (Pratt's essential "Arts of the Contact Zone," Guy Allen's account of his "Writing Experiment at the University of Toronto"), students (Mauk's "Location, Location, Location," Sommers and Saltz's report on her longitudinal study of Harvard students), and teaching grammar and voice. Students enjoy reading Jeffrey Maxson's updating/translation of Pratt, "'Government of da Peeps'" in week nine and trying out ideas for cultural studies classrooms. In class, we brainstorm for various metaphors for a classroom and then I ask them what they could "do next" with this activity. Jennie Nelson's "Reading Classrooms as Text" in week ten is my perennial challenge to their assumptions about what students bring to a writing class and a model of double consciousness of student and teacher perspectives, especially in creating writing assignments. I bring teaching identity to the foreground in week eleven, with the title, "Transformations." Here, Alison Cook-Sather, Dawn Skorczewski, and Jacqueline Jones Royster variously help us think about the roles we play, the assumptions we make, and the changes we undergo as students and teachers. Royster's "When the First Voice You Hear is Not Your Own" provides a segue into week twelve and Fan Shen's "The Classroom and the Wider Culture" as we confront questions about teaching grammar and acknowledge rhetorical positions—and voices—of Others in the classroom.

As we engage in such professional dialogue, most students quite naturally begin to speak in class as teachers ("I think we need to help students discover...") rather than as students ("I didn't learn brainstorming in school."). To reinforce this transformative process and help students toward a more self-reflective way of thinking about teaching—and learning—I ask them to write a self-assessment when they submit their collections of weekly reading response pieces, noting their emerging approach to teaching and their progress over weeks of reading and thinking. Students also write reflections on their writing and revision of the two major essays, not only to help them develop awareness of themselves as learners but also to promote critical thinking about the processes and products of teaching. The prompts ask class members to go beyond reflecting on what they do to examine what our course does, to look at assignments and their outcomes.

Thus from the first class meeting, LIT 730 welcomes students "behind the scenes," positioning them as teachers analyzing pedagogical strategies rather than as students in the usual outsider audience position. I seek to stimulate what Donna Qualley has called a "reflexive stance," aiming prompts, readings, and class activities to involve students in "a dialectical engagement with the other—an other idea, theory, person, culture, text, or even an other part of one's self" (11). I step back from teaching moments during class to review them like snapshots in a digital camera. We talk about the hunches, hopes, and mistakes that guided my choices for the course. Students have an opportunity to look at my teaching through the lens of their learning so that we become partners in this enterprise of learning about teaching. Comments from former students who are now teachers suggest that this approach plays a positive role in fostering thoughtful, reflective practice.

A few years ago, a bit of metacognitive description in one of these student reflections caught my attention. The writer succinctly described what I had designed as "a course about a course." Now, as I have turned more and more toward explicitly teaching the course "about itself," challenging students to participate with double vision and self-awareness, I see the reflexive mode must do double duty as an approach to student learning and a part of (my) teacher learning as well.

Critical Reflection

For the teacher of this course, as much as the students, awareness of what happens in classrooms feeds into what happens in this particular class. The teacher must fearlessly open her/his practice to examination, just as students must probe their past experiences in education, to determine what works, what doesn't, and why. The teaching class becomes our experiment in how a classroom operates. It's a scary, risky, and exhilarating way to teach a class.

The course continues to evolve around my main challenges in teaching it: the relationship to/with theory, the dialogue with current conversations in the profession, and the self-reflective awareness of moves and motivations in teaching. In my brief class lectures, I find myself favoring Friere one semester, focusing more on Bakhtin another, playing up rhetorical roots sometimes and emphasizing postmodern affinities other times. But the reading list is often the focus for my tweaking, as I wrestle with weaknesses in offering an overview of the shifting currents of our professional conversations.

One glaring gap is the dearth of material about teaching and technology in my syllabus. It stems partly from the inevitable obsolescence of much published material and partly from the lack of time and space in the schedule to do justice to this increasingly important topic. For students whose lives are entwined with digital technology, my efforts to include "relevant" reading have often fallen flat. More successful have been our forays online to conduct class activities. The electronic discussion board on Blackboard has proved an acceptable venue for the reading responses in the second half of the semester. Three or four students responsible for the week's prompts open threads, and the responders can see each others' posts.

I brought my concerns about the lack of "tech talk" to colleagues in our College Writing Program, some of whom are graduates of LIT 730. Several suggested meeting new teachers' needs to learn about teaching with technology by incorporating hands-on experience and experimentation into their course work. So I assign students to consider how they can use classroom applications—from the old overhead projector to Powerpoint projection and video—as they lead discussions and make presentations. Since most of my students are "digital natives" and I am not, I hope that challenging them to take the lead will naturally bring technology into class discussion, raise their awareness of the need for making conscious classroom choices, and encourage them to connect their everyday online literacies with their teaching practice.

Another syllabus drawback I have wrestled with involves multicultural issues. It is difficult to avoid isolating discussion of second language writers, for example, in a designated week when we read articles like Fan Shen's "The Classroom and the Wider Culture" and talk about teaching grammar and style. Dissatisfied with this conventionally Othering approach, I have sought advice from our writing program's international student counselor to integrate ideas about language and cultural difference throughout the course. I have introduced ideas about contrastive rhetoric, for example, into our opening discussion of literacy. Now I am working toward putting such syllabus design issues in front of rather than behind the scenes. I hope that if such syllabus choices can be discussed openly, students can bring their own perspectives on—and experience with—difference into the discussion. But the problem of where and when to raise issues of grammar, style, and voice keeps me rearranging the syllabus from year to year.

Finally, the lack of a widely-accepted template for teaching composition provides a puzzle for instructors and students in this course. Such indeterminacy is at once stylishly postmodern and fiendishly frustrating for students still wedded to the traditional way that academic institutions present learning as finding a set of "right answers." As Christine Farris warns, in our efforts to present the variety of new ideas in teaching composition, "we may find ourselves handing new teachers postmodern tools to do what is institutionally configured as a modern job" (99). In addition, the very reflexivity that fascinates me in this enterprise can discourage students who arrive inadequately prepared for such intellectual acrobatics. While I blithely goad my students to "read the course as a text" (about itself!), my own reading of the course syllabus raises difficult questions about my handling of Composition's code words and conventions. Examining the (attached) LIT 730 syllabus through students' eyes, I see that I am expecting them to enter a "conversation" with strangers who are scholars of a previously unknown discipline, to discover the difference between teaching as a verb and pedagogy as a noun (ie. turn an activity into an object of study), and to learn a new vocabulary—in some ways, take on a new identity.

No wonder they sometimes write about feeling overwhelmed.

And perhaps the biggest challenge for me in teaching this course comes from its very call for a reflexive stance: this course about a course demands double consciousness from its instructor as well as its students. Farris suggests a possible response to this challenge: we can "try to make visible the teaching moves we would like to see [students] making—just as we would make academic writing and cultural analysis moves visible to first-year undergraduates who might not intuit or invent them on their own" (102).

So I will continue to try to define what I'm doing in this course more explicitly, making the theoretical underpinnings of the course more transparent and showing students explicitly how the course operates. For example, future iterations of the weekly response prompts could include explanations of *why* the questions ask them to look at texts in certain ways and bring their own experience to bear in responding to reading. An explicit link between the "moves" we make in academic writing (as Graff and Birkenstein put it) and teaching choices as a matter of "moves" may help students cross the intellectual bridge from seeing classes as a student to thinking like a teacher.

Note

1. All quotations from student work, while anonymous, are used with permission.

Works Cited

Allen, Guy. "Language, Power, and Consciousness: A Writing Experiment at the University of Toronto." Johnson 65-98. Print.

Baron, Naomi. "Gresham's Ghost: Challenges to Written Culture." *Always On: Language in an Online and Mobile World.* New York: Oxford UP, 2008. 183-212. Print.

Bartholomae, David. "Inventing the University." Johnson 2-31. Print.

Belanger, Kelly, and Sibylle Gruber. "Unraveling Generative Tensions in the Composition Practicum." *Don't Call it That: The Composition Practicum.* Ed. Sidney I. Dobrin. Urbana: NCTE, 2005.113-40. Print.

Berlin, James. "Rhetoric and Ideology in the Writing Class." Johnson 117-37. Print.

Berthoff, Ann. "From *The Making of Meaning.*" Johnson 292-304. Print.

Cook-Sather, Alison. "Education as Translation: Students Transforming Notions of Narrative and Self." *CCC* 55.1 (2003): 91-114. Print.

Corbett, Edward P.J., Nancy Myers, and Gary Tate. *The Writing Teacher's Sourcebook.* 4th ed. New York: Oxford UP, 2000. Print.

Dave, Anish M., and David R. Russell. "Drafting and Revision Using Word Processing by Undergraduate Student Writers: Changing Conceptions and Practices." *Research in the Teaching of English* 44.4 (2010): 406-34. Print.

Elbow, Peter. "Closing My Eyes as I Speak: An Argument for Ignoring Audience." Johnson 172-94. Print.

Farris, Christine. "Too Cool for School? Composition as Cultural Studies and Reflective Practice." *Preparing College Teachers of Writing: Histories, Theories, Programs, Practices.* Ed. Betty P. Pytlik and Sarah Liggett. New York: Oxford UP, 2002. 97-107. Print.

Graff, Gerald. "From *Clueless in Academe.*" Johnson 32-58. Print.

Graff, Gerald, and Cathy Birkenstein. *They Say/I Say: the Moves that Matter in Academic Writing.* 2nd ed. New York: W.W. Norton & Co, 2010. Print.

Harris, Joseph. "Opinion: Revision as a Critical Practice." *College English* 65.6 (2003): 577-92. Print.

Hesse, Douglas. "Teachers as Students, Reflecting Resistance." *CCC* 44.2 (1993): 224–31. Print.

Johnson, T.R., ed. *Teaching Composition: Background Readings.* 3rd ed. Boston: Bedford/St. Martin's, 2008. Print.

Kameen, Paul. *Writing/Teaching: Essays Toward a Rhetoric of Pedagogy.* Pittsburgh: U Pittsburgh P, 2000. Print.

Lindemann, Erika. *A Rhetoric for Writing Teachers.* 3rd ed. New York: Oxford UP, 1995. Print.

Mauk, Johnathan. "Location, Location, Location: The 'Real' (E)states of Being, Writing, and Thinking in Composition." *College English* 65.4 (2003): 368-88. Print.

Maxson, Jeffrey. "'Government of da Peeps, for da Peeps, and by da Peeps': Revisiting the Contact Zone." *Journal of Basic Writing* 24.1 (2005): 24-47. Print.

Nelson, Jennie. "Reading Classrooms as Text: Exploring Student Writers' Interpretive Practices." *CCC* 46. 3 (1995): 411-29. Print.

Perl, Sondra. "Understanding Composing." Johnson 140-47. Print.

Plato. *Phaedrus*. Trans. Walter Hamilton. New York: Penguin, 1973. *Digital Humanities*. Web. 15 Aug. 2010.

Pratt, Mary Louise. "Arts of the Contact Zone." *Profession 91*. New York: MLA, 1991. 33-40. Print.

Qualley, Donna. *Turns of Thought: Teaching Composition as Reflexive Inquiry*. Portsmouth: Heinemann, 1997. Print.

Rankin, Elizabeth. *Seeing Yourself as a Teacher: Conversations with Five New Teachers in a University Writing Program*. Urbana: NCTE, 1994. Print.

Reid, E. Shelley. "Uncoverage in Composition Pedagogy." *Composition Studies* 32.1 (2004): 15–34. Print.

Rose, Mike. "I Just Wanna Be Average." *Lives on the Boundary: The Struggles and Achievements Of America's Underprepared*. New York: Free P, 1989. 11-38. Print.

---. "Rigid Rules, Inflexible Plans, and the Stifling of Language: A Cognitivist Analysis of Writer's Block." Johnson 148-62. Print.

Royster, Jacqueline Jones. "When the First Voice You Hear Is Not Your Own." *CCC* 47.1 (1996): 29-40. Print.

Shen, Fan. "The Classroom and the Wider Culture: Identity as a Key to Learning English Composition." *CCC* 40.4 (1989): 459-66. Print.

Skorczewski, Dawn. "From Playing the Role to Being Yourself: Becoming the Teacher in the Writing Classroom." Johnson 99-116. Print.

Sommers, Nancy. "Across the Drafts." *CCC* 58.2 (2006): 248-56. Print.

Sommers, Nancy, and Laura Saltz. "The Novice as Expert: Writing the Freshman Year." *CCC* 56.1 (2004): 124-49. Print.

Stancliff, Michael, and Maureen Daly Goggin. "What's Theorizing Got to Do With It? Teaching Theory as Resourceful Conflict and Reflection in TA Preparation." *Writing Program Administration* 30.3 (2007): 11-28. Web. 19 July 2010.

Yancey, Kathleen Blake. "Writing in the 21st Century: A Report from the National Council of Teachers of English." Urbana: NCTE, 2009. Web. 10 Aug. 2010.

Appendix

Teaching Composition
LIT 730

Janet Gebhart Auten
Office: 228 Battelle
[The Writing Center]
Office Hours Mon. 3:00-5:00

Welcome. This teaching seminar is an introduction to **Composition Studies,** a field that includes the history, theory, and teaching of writing. It explores the nature of written language and the theoretical, social, and cultural contexts of teaching composition. You will discover spirited debates about *why* we teach, *how* we teach, and *what* we teach—academic writing. [Please note: this is not a "methods" course. Our focus will be on foundations rather than fundamentals of conducting a class.]

Course Goals

Through your work in the course, you can expect to

- better understand the way individuals construct—and are constructed by—writing.
- get an introduction to the field of Composition Studies, including principles of rhetoric and linguistics, theories of composition, teaching, and learning.
- understand the dynamics and demands of written discourse, of academic literacy, of the writing classroom.
- get a variety of perspectives on ways composition courses can be to designed and implemented; understand the major pedagogies used to teach composition.
- discuss the issues and strategies involved in assigning and evaluating writing and helping students carry out academic writing assignments successfully.
- refine your own command of the writing process and of academic writing through constant critical writing in a variety of modes and genres.

Course Texts

Like most other LIT courses, this class rests on *regular—and substantial—reading.*

T. R. Johnson, ed. *Teaching Composition: Background Readings.* 3rd ed. Boston: Bedford/ St. Martin's, 2008. Print.

Good news! This book of readings is provided free by the publisher. (I'll have them for you at the first class meeting.)

Please purchase:

Graff, Gerald, and Cathy Birkenstein, *They Say/I Say: the Moves that Matter in Academic Writing.* 2nd ed. New York: W.W. Norton & Co, 2010. Print. (about $16 on Amazon).

Additional articles are provided online [on Blackboard*].

Evaluation
Your grade in the course will be determined by your work on
1. Collected responses to reading   (2 – 25% each)   **50%**
2. Essay on academic literacy   **20%**
3. Analysis essay and presentation   **20%**
4. Class participation/group work/leading class discussion   **10%**

1. Reading response   [50% of course grade]

This reflective writing component is the heart of the course, the place where you explore and analyze the course material. You will *respond* to questions on the week's readings (I write the prompts for first half; you write them in the second half of the semester). This is an important way of thinking through academic writing that we use in teaching as well. My reading and commenting in response to your responses allows us to establish a professional dialogue—*in writing*—that enhances the course for us both. You should submit your response either electronically or on paper by class time each week.

Evaluation: I'm looking for quality not quantity—but most people need 5-6 pages to create an adequate discussion. Please feel free to write your way into the reading, but then go back and prune it down to 5 pages or so.

The weekly responses are ***not*** graded individually but collectively—thus, you'll have an opportunity to revise and submit them as a portfolio at midterm and at semester's end.

2. Writing/research/teaching projects*   [40% of course grade]

1.) Autobiographical essay   5-7 pages.
What is the path by which you developed academic literacy? To what extent does your own experience illustrate and/or give insight into the issues we have been talking and reading about in class? Based on your own experience and observation, write an essay engaging in the conversation about how "academic literacy" is taught in colleges and universities.

Due in Week 6, this essay represents your personal exploration of academic literacy.

It asks you to mine your *own* experience of learning academic writing in order to examine and understand your attitudes, assumptions, and outlook as a teacher of academic writing, then draw out the larger implications of your experience with reference to course reading.

**Revision: You may revise the graded essay and resubmit a new version with the original within 5 weeks. I'll give it a <u>second grade</u> which is averaged with the first.

2.) Analysis essay and presentation   6-8 pages
This essay responds to one of four "provocations"—quotations from

composition scholars that speak to issues, theories, scholars you'll encounter in the course.

You'll pick one topic and discuss it, based on ideas you have developed during the semester as well as reading/research in two or three articles chosen from recent issues of our professional journals [eg. *College English, College Composition and Communication, Composition Studies, Kairos* (online), and so on].

You'll prepare a lesson plan and give a 15-min. presentation and a handout.

This assignment offers an opportunity to synthesize course material, read recent scholarship, and formulate your own ideas about a particular topic, then "teach" it.

* [Note: we'll talk more about these writing assignments as we go]

3. Participation [10% of course grade]

Of course, your engagement is assumed and expected—but here are details anyway.

Attendance is a must. Your presence and participation in class are crucial to the success of this seminar. If for some reason you must be absent one week, please make sure to contact me *and* a classmate so that we can at least see that you get notes.

Group work: As you will learn in this course, collaborative learning is very important in writing pedagogy. You're expected to engage in "peer response" and other group work.

Leading discussion: In week 2 of the course, I'll ask you to sign up to lead the discussion on the readings one week. We'll have 2 leaders per class, so if you see a particular topic or want to sign up with someone, be ready to do so in the 2nd week.

4. Course Expectations

To teach at the college level, you'll need to be able to demonstrate knowledge of the discipline, make sound decisions in pedagogy, write clear, coherent academic prose yourself, and share in a scholarly community. It is my conviction that the best preparation for teaching writing in the academy involves plentiful practice in reading and writing the genres you will be teaching: the essay, rhetorical analysis, and scholarly argument.

This class involves a high *level* of reading—and a different *kind of reading* than that found in most other literature classes. It consists of the varied, important, and sometimes challenging analytical articles that have helped to shape our discipline over the past 40 years. One thing that our anthology obscures is the origin of these articles. They have all been published, discussed, and often debated in the profession, usually in the pages of our two main journals, *College Composition and Communication* and *College English*. Both journals are published by the National Council of Teachers of English (NCTE)—a professional organization which you'll want to become acquainted with [www.ncte.org].

Some advice on the course reading from previous students:

- Be prepared to take notes as you read and re-read. Note especially the key terms. Look for ways an article works, not just what it "says."
- *Slow down your reading.* These texts require a different level of attention than that novel you have to read in a week or an article in the newspaper.
- Avoid the freshman last-minute syndrome that you'll have to address with your students. Give yourself time to read and reflect on reading before you respond.

5. A final word about the course...

This is a course about a course: We will be using our own class as a laboratory where we try out strategies and try to ground abstract ideas in concrete reality. It is a chance to observe "behind the curtain." I leave it to you to begin to observe closely—and not just in our class!—and to begin to formulate some ideas about *how classes work.*

Teaching Composition   Reading/ Assignment Schedule

Sources: T.R. Johnson, *Teaching Composition: Background Readings,* 3rd ed. (R); Blackboard (B)
[Note: chapters from Graff and Birkenstein won't figure in response papers (G&B)]

To Prepare For **Week 2: Teaching the Academy**, read and respond to:
- David Bartholomae, "Inventing the University" (R)
- Gerald Graff, from *Clueless in Academe* (R)
- Mike Rose, "I Just Wanna Be Average" (B)
- Kathleen B. Yancey, "Writing in the 21st Century" (B)
Response paper due by class time
G&B, Preface, Intro and Chpt. 12 *"Reading for the Conversation"*

To Prepare For **Week 3: Teaching Literacy**, read and respond to:
- Naomi Baron, "Gresham's Ghost" (B)
- Plato, "Phaedrus" (excerpt) (B)
- Lisa Delpit, "The Politics of Teaching Literate Discourse" (R)
Response paper due by class time
G&B Part I, Chpt. 1-3

To Prepare For **Week 4: Looking at Composing**, read and respond to:
- Sondra Perl, "Understanding Composing" (R)
- Mike Rose, "Rigid Rules, Inflexible Plans, and the Stifling of Language: A Cognitivist Analysis of Writer's Block" (R)

- Anish Dave and David Russell, "Drafting and Revision..." (B)
Response paper due by class time

To Prepare For **Week 5: Teaching the Process: Invention**, read and respond to:
- Ann Berthoff, from *The Making of Meaning* (R)
- Peter Elbow, "Closing My Eyes as I Speak: An Argument for Ignoring Audience" (R)
G&B Part 2, Chpt 4-7
Bring full draft of Essay #1 * (3 copies) - no response paper due

To Prepare For **Week 6: Teaching the Process: Revision**, read and respond to:
- Nancy Sommers, "Revision Strategies of Student Writers and Experienced Adult Writers" (R)
- Joseph Harris, "Revision as Critical Practice" (B)
Autobiographical essay due *(5-7 pages)*
The development of academic writing—your experience as example
1-2 page revision reflection with paper—no response paper

To Prepare For **Week 7: Teaching the Process: Evaluation**, read and respond to:
- Peter Elbow, "Ranking, Evaluating, Liking: Sorting Out Three Forms of Judgment" (R)
- Nancy Sommers, "Responding to Student Writing" (R) and "Across the Drafts" (B)
- Andrea Muldoon, "A Case for Critical Revision" (B)
 Review 2 videos on commenting and evaluate sample papers (B)

To Prepare For **Week 8: Debating Pedagogy**, read and respond to:
- James Berlin, "Rhetoric and Ideology in the Writing Class" (R)
- David Bartholomae, "...Without Teachers," and Elbow, "Being a Writer..." (B)
G&B Chpt 11, "I Take Your Point"
Hand in collection of 3 responses (originals + revisions) and 1-2 pp reflection.

To Prepare For **Week 9: Re-vising Pedagogy**, read and respond to:
- Guy Allen, "Language, Power, and Consciousness: A Writing Experiment at the University of Toronto" (R)
- Mary Louise Pratt, "Arts of the Contact Zone" (B)
- Jeffrey Maxson, "Govt. of da Peeps ... Revisiting the Contact Zone" (B)
Post response/question on Blackboard

To Prepare For **Week 10: Students**, read and respond to:
- Johnathan Mauk, "Location, Location, Location" (B)
- Jennie Nelson, "Reading Classrooms as Texts" (B)

- Sommers and Saltz, "Novice as Expert: Writing the Freshman Year" (B)
Post response/question on Blackboard

To Prepare For **Week 11: Transformations**, read and respond to:
- Alison Cook-Sather, "Education as Translation" (B)
- Dawn Skorczewski, "From Playing the Role to Being Yourself: Becoming the Teacher in the Writing Classroom" (R)
- Jacqueline Jones Royster, "When the First Voice You Hear ..." (B)
Post response/question on Blackboard

To Prepare For **Week 12: Language/Voice**, read and respond to:
- Fan Shen, "The Classroom and the Wider Culture" (B)
- Bonnie Devet, "Welcoming Grammar Back..." (B)
- Wayne Booth, "The Rhetorical Stance" (R)
G&B Part 3, Chpts 8-10
Schedule a paper conference with me this week; no response due

To Prepare For **Week 13: Courses and Classrooms**, read and respond to:
- Elizabeth Wardle, "Mutt Genres" (B)
G&B, Chpt. 14, "Analyze This"
In Class: "Inside the Teachers' Studio" – College Writing faculty panel
"Hand in" collected response posts (originals + revisions) and 1-2 pp reflection.

To Prepare For **Week 14: Presentations – Joining the Conversation**, bring one-page handout or abstract of a recent article to share

To Prepare For **Week 15: Presentations – Joining the Conversation**
- Critical analysis essay (6-8 pages) "Joining the Conversation about Teaching Writing" due

Readings Available on Blackboard

Baron, Naomi. "Gresham's Ghost: Challenges to Written Culture." *Always On: Language in an Online and Mobile World*. New York: Oxford UP, 2008. 183-212. Print.

Bartholomae, David. "Writing with Teachers: A Conversation with Peter Elbow." *CCC* 46.1 (1995): 62-71. Print.

Booth, Wayne. "The Rhetorical Stance." *Teaching Composition: Background Readings*. Ed. T.R. Johnson. 3rd ed. Boston: Bedford/St. Martin's, 2008. 163-72. Print.

Cook-Sather, Alison. "Education as Translation: Students Transforming Notions of Narrative and Self." *CCC* 55.1 (2003): 91-114. Print.

Dave, Anish M., and David R. Russell. "Drafting and Revision Using Word Processing by Undergraduate Student Writers: Changing Conceptions and Practices." *Research in the Teaching of English* 44.4 (2010): 406-34. Print.

Delpit, Lisa. "The Politics of Teaching Literate Discourse." *Teaching Composition: Background Readings.* Ed. T.R. Johnson. 3rd ed. Boston: Bedford/St. Martin's, 2008. 491-502. Print.

Devet, Bonnie. "Welcoming Grammar Back into the Writing Classroom." *Teaching English in the Two-Year College* (2002): 8-17. Print.

Elbow, Peter. "Being a Writer vs. Being an Academic: A Conflict in Goals." *CCC* 46.1 (1995): 72-83. Print.

Harris, Joseph. "Opinion: Revision as a Critical Practice." *College English* 65.6 (2003): 577-92. Print.

Mauk, Johnathan. "Location, Location, Location: The 'Real' (E)states of Being, Writing, and Thinking in Composition." *College English* 65.4 (2003): 368-88. Print.

Maxson, Jeffrey. "'Government of da Peeps, for da Peeps, and by da Peeps': Revisiting the Contact Zone." *Journal of Basic Writing* 24.1 (2005): 24-47. Print.

Muldoon, Andrea. "A Case for Critical Revision: Debunking the Myth of the Enlightened Teacher versus the Resistant Student Writer." *College Teaching* 57.2 (2009): 67-71. Print.

Nelson, Jennie. "Reading Classrooms as Text: Exploring Student Writers' Interpretive Practices." *CCC* 46.3 (1995): 411-29. Print.

Plato. *Phaedrus.* Trans. Walter Hamilton. New York: Penguin, 1973. *Digital Humanities.* Web. 15 Aug. 2010.

Pratt, Mary Louise. "Arts of the Contact Zone." *Profession 91.* New York: MLA, 1991. 33-40. Print.

Rose, Mike. "I Just Wanna Be Average." *Lives on the Boundary: The Struggles and Achievements of America's Underprepared.* New York: Free P, 1989. 11-38. Print.

Royster, Jacqueline Jones. "When the First Voice You Hear Is Not Your Own." *CCC* 47.1 (1996) 29-40. Print.

Shen, Fan. "The Classroom and the Wider Culture: Identity as a Key to Learning English Composition." *CCC* 40.4 (1989): 459-66. Print.

Sommers, Nancy. "Across the Drafts." *CCC* 58.2 (2006): 248-56. Print.

Sommers, Nancy and Laura Saltz. "The Novice as Expert: Writing the Freshman Year." *CCC* 56.1 (2004): 124-49. Print.

Wardle, Elizabeth. "'Mutt Genres' and the Goal of FYC: Can We Help Students Write the Genres of the University?" *CCC* 60.4 (2009): 765-89. Print.

Yancey, Kathleen Blake. "2008 NCTE Presidential Address: The Impulse to Compose and the Age of Composition." *Research in the Teaching of English* 43.3 (2009): 316-38. Print.

Narrative Inquiry: Approaches to Language and Literacy Research, by David Schaafsma and Ruth Vinz. New York: Teachers College P, 2011. 146 pp.

Reviewed by Jaqueline McLeod Rogers, University of Winnipeg

When I first looked at Schaafsma and Vinz's *On Narrative Inquiry*, I set it aside several times as oversimplified and under theorized, even a bit gawky in its insistent use of narrative frameworks to explicate the theory and practice of narrative research. Metaphor gets awkwardly out of hand in an early chapter, for example, when Burkean parlor shape-shifts into a fishing boat large enough to hold a crew of orators angrily contesting the definition of narrative (19-22). Yet readers who persevere are rewarded, because the authors eventually accomplish the important task of illuminating their central question: "What is the research in narrative?" (3).

At heart, the book is a practical how-to guide encouraging an option-based form of narrative inquiry. The authors wrote five of the nine chapters, and in these, move through issues roughly in the order that they might be expected to arise in a flexible inquiry process. The early chapters provide a literature review of narrative inquiry in education research, while later chapters take up issues such as how to identify story strands, how to acknowledge and manage researcher subjectivity, and how to deliberate amongst the options for crafting stories.

The book begins by offering a brief history of contemporary uses of the term "narrative," locating it in Russian formalism, modernist structuralism, and then postmodernism to indicate how it has changed meaning over the past century. While the authors allude to the expansiveness of the term, they never quite capture its reach like David Herman does in a recent book, when he characterizes it "as a cognitive structure or way of making sense ... as a type of text ... and as a resource for communicative interaction" (7). Of course, Schaafsma and Vinz have a particular interest in narrative inquiry as applied to education research in language and literacy, but even with the focus thus refined they contend there is still no consensus. To bring provisional clarity, they propose a narrative inquiry that typically makes these four moves:

1. Makes visible the puzzles of mind—framings, evidences, stances, theories, and questions in the researcher's composing of the text.
2. Challenges its own questions, answers, possibilities and theories.
3. Grapples with issues of responsibility, power, relations, and ethics as it evidences the importance of learning with others.
4. Works to redefine the products or outcomes of research. (8)

While they discuss these moves throughout the nine chapters, they feature centrally in the telling of chapter 5. In this chapter, the story builds around the self-reflective practices of Rashid, a young teacher in the Bronx who questions why his high school students remain disconnected from poetry discussions. He is participating as one of several teachers in Paul's doctoral study aimed at composing "a tapestry of English teachers' stories about how they enact their beliefs about literacy curriculum and instructional practices" (70). Yet rather than helping to weave this pretty pattern, Rashid's reflections not only capture his unease as a teacher, but also provoke Paul to express similar insecurity and Ruth, in the role of dissertation advisor, to write a discouraging teaching evaluation. This story about teaching troubles has no easy or happy ending. Rashid also asks questions about the process of narrative inquiry, by which he interrogates his practice. He records both a dawning recognition that his questions elude answers, and concerns about a research process that allows researchers to decide what to tell—"Will any story do? ... Who controls the research agenda, questions, and the stories that get told?" (68).

At this stage in chapter 5, Schaafsma and Vinz propose three lenses to help researchers examine decisions about what gets told: salience (what stands out and stays with you?), incompleteness (where are the gaps?), and emphasis (are there patterns of repetition that suggest a focus?) (78-79). Looking through these lenses is not a procedure that eliminates subjectivity, but a way to make provisional decisions about focus and focalization. To make other moves toward compensating for subjectivity and interpretation, researchers can situate themselves in the story and ask direct questions about how their responses to the current situation may be filtered through prior experiences and views. They can include multiple angles of vision and relevant critical theory and work to draw readers in with meta-narrative explaining design choices. In sum, the authors recommend portraying research-in-process as open-ended and generative, never as proposing final answers (68, 79).

There is the practical question of how to apply this book to scholarship and teaching in the area of composition studies. In classes that call for and examine the personal essay, creative non-fiction, and even the methodology of narrative inquiry, it would be difficult to assign the book in its entirety as a course text because it focuses so squarely on educational questions. For my students, most of the discussion issues and examples of classroom pedagogy would not easily transfer to exploring questions about writing matters and social discourse.

Yet excerpts from the book could illuminate certain standard assignments. For example, following a model used in many first-year composition courses, I ask my students to write a personal narrative essay as a first assignment. In our post-expressivist classrooms, such an assignment requires students to move beyond simply recounting a memory, and instead to reflect on possible perspectives and meanings; as Candace Spigelman notes, "narrative argument" needs to be *"purposeful* and intended to do more than express opinion or cathartically confess" (6). One of the ways to cultivate argument and establish purpose is to introduce an outside source or theory. To see how this can be done, most students need a model, and there is an excellent one at the end of chapter 5, in a student-written narrative that connects seeing a sign that says "Keep off the grass" with Bourdieu's theory of *habitus*. The essay is short, well written and insightful. By reading it, students can see how experience and theory can interact to be mutually illuminating.

At a more advanced undergraduate level, I teach a course called "Narrative Thinking and Writing," a unit of which is dedicated to studying oral history and telling others' lives. To support this work, students could benefit from examining chapters 6, 7, and 8 as a package. Chapters 6 and 8 reproduce some of the dissertation work Randi Dickson did to narrate the lives of four outstanding teachers. In chapter 6, there are notes and journal entries that capture Dickson's thorough observations of two of her subjects, Mona and Sue. Whereas students could consult methods books for more abstract discussions of observation and field note techniques, Dickson's notes effectively show the process in progress.

Chapter 7, by authors Schaafsma and Vinz, provides a more step-by-step discussion of some of the techniques writers can use to form their narratives, alerting them to making choices about the author's role in the story, about the author's relation to the audience in terms of sharing writing decisions, about bringing subjects to life, and about the role of time. Following this, we return in chapter 8 to passages of Dickson's narrative about Mona, which is interspersed with commentary about crafting choices. Dickson points out that it is difficult to showcase her subject's teaching talents, for Mona is now long retired and struggles in interviews to remember the details of her teaching life, let alone recreate vibrant moments (121). Dickson describes the choices she made to attempt to overcome these perspectival limits, yet avoids false optimism by acknowledging at chapter end that the narrative text will not be able to capture the full richness of the subject (122).

As a researcher who has puzzled questions about the ethos of personal voice writing and the value of narrative as evidence, I was impressed by the tenacity with which the authors of the book pressed the question, "what can be learned from narrating or reading [stories]?" (3). Like Dewey who inspires this work, the authors believe that the journey is as valuable as the destination—that rather than proving a point, they are learning as they go.

Winnipeg, MB, Canada

Works Cited

Herman, David. *Basic Elements of Narrative*. West Sussex: Wiley-Blackwell, 2009. Print.

Spigelman, Candace. *Personally Speaking: Experience as Evidence in Academic Discourse*. Carbondale: Southern Illinois UP, 2004. Print.

Everyday Genres: Writing Assignments across the Disciplines, by Mary Soliday. Carbondale: Southern Illinois UP, 2011. 151 pp.

Reviewed By Irene L. Clark, California State University

In 1993, I spent three months at the University of Utrecht teaching a course in academic writing to students who were completing PhD work in the field of geography. My students had enjoyed significant academic success and were deeply committed to their chosen field. Most spoke several languages, their English was excellent, and they wanted very much to achieve the stated goal of the course—to write a potentially publishable article in English based on their research. However, when I received the first drafts of their articles, I was surprised and puzzled to note a problem that I didn't anticipate. The problem had nothing to do with grammatical or syntactical error, word choice, or even the unfamiliar structural strategies characteristic of texts written by English Language Learners. Rather, the problem was exactly the one I encounter each semester in the writing of first year students in the United States and often in the writing of upper division and graduate students as well—there was no main point, no thesis, no unifying theme. Apparently, neither my Dutch nor my American students were aware of the underlying purpose of academic writing—to address an exigence, that is, a defect, an obstacle, a gap, or a problem, on which to base an argument and which would provide focus and unity in the text. Because my Dutch students did not have what in current genre scholarship is referred to as "genre awareness," their writing consisted primarily of detailed summaries of research presented in no particular order. There was no argument or unifying premise.

It was at that time that I first encountered scholarship concerned with the reconceptualized theory of genre, the work of John Swales and Amy Devitt, in particular, and I found that when I applied insights derived from that theory to my teaching at Utrecht, my students' writing improved significantly. Since that time, genre theory has been a significant presence in my scholarship and teaching; I have found that when students, both graduate and undergraduate, acquire "genre awareness," they are able to navigate the expectations of academic writing with success and to approach new genres effectively.

How delighted I am, then, to read Mary Soliday's slim, but insightful book, *Everyday Genres: Writing Assignments across the Disciplines*, which applies insights from rhetorical genre theory in a WAC context. The book recounts Soliday's experience at the City College of New York (CCNY), in which doctoral students, called Writing Fellows, were paired with faculty in several disciplines to enable faculty to improve their teaching in general education courses, major courses, and some graduate courses, a related goal being to enable students to write appropriately in particular disciplinary contexts. Soliday views the concept of genre as a means of helping content professors clarify their own rhetorical understanding and raises what is becoming a seminal WAC oriented question: how can we help students apply what they know about writing across new situations and contexts? Is it possible to do so? In addition, Soliday raises a second equally important question: "What is a good assignment?" She concludes that, "because genre is a social practice, an assignment must be aligned with the social motives the genre performs for readers" (11).

Soliday situates her book within a particular set of experiences associated with the CUNY-Wide WAC Mandate, which implemented a program in which writing fellows worked with faculty in several disciplines: Anthropology, Early Childhood Development, Music Appreciation, Art, and Biology. The book consists of an Introduction, three chapters, a conclusion and an appendix that contains reflective statements by content faculty, attests to the success of the program, and explains the strategies and insights into assignment development that the program enabled them to learn. Chapter 1, titled "Sharing Genre Expertise," traces how the Writing Fellows worked with the faculty to implement the program, focusing on the useful concept of "teacher talk"—that is, how teachers across disciplines *talk* about and evaluate student writing as they craft "prompts, guidelines, warnings in class, commentary on papers" (12). Soliday refers to "teacher talk" as a university metagenre, of which successful students are aware when they compose, but which can also be confusing for students, particularly when it contains contradictory instructions, such as when teachers urge students to use their own voices and then caution them to use appropriately formal language. Soliday maintains that confusion in this metagenre is inherent in academic writing, because an expert stance consists of one's own perspective combined with the words of others, a creative blend that involves a complex understanding that novices to the academy rarely have.

Chapter 2, "Stance in Genre," considers how writers achieve authority to speak about evidence in university genres. Drawing on interviews, Soliday focuses on the importance of teacher talk in helping students understand what constitutes evidence in a given discipline, noting that academically proficient students were able to fulfill their readers' expectations by assimilating the teacher's words, not copying them, achieving the distinction between imitation and typicality that constitutes genre appropriateness. Chapter 3, "Content in Genre," uses the theory of Jean Lave and Etienne Wenger to consider how writers find ideas and facts and turn their material into evidence for readers. It contrasts what researchers know about writing genres in the workplace with the standard teaching of genre across the curriculum.

The strategies and reflections associated with this project are thought-provoking and useful unto themselves. But what I found most important is Soliday's discussion of transferability—that is, the extent to which generic academic writing, as taught in a first year writing class, can help students grapple with assignments across the curriculum. This is the conundrum of genre study, an issue that continues to generate scholarly disagreement (see in particular, Petraglia's 1995 collection *Reconceiving Writing, Rethinking Writing Instruction* and Thaiss and Zawacki's 2006 study *Engaged Writers, Dynamic Disciplines*). David Russell maintains that general writing instruction that is not linked to a discipline is like teaching a course in general ball-handling and then expecting students to be equally proficient in such varied games as baseball, football, basketball, tennis, and jacks; writing, Russell emphasizes is situated within activity systems (55). More recently, a study of a large mid western composition program, conducted by Elizabeth Wardle, maintains the difficulty of teaching academic writing genres in only one context (see "'Mutt Genres'"). Wardle's study questions the existence of autonomous writing and the possibility of teaching students transferable skills, whereas Gerald Graff, in *Clueless in Academe*, maintains that "one of the most closely guarded secrets that academia unwittingly keeps from students and everybody else is that all academics, despite their many differences, play a version of the same game of *persuasive argument*." Graff acknowledges that although each discipline has its own version, each is a form of what he refers to as "arguespeak" (22).

Soliday, countering Paul Prior's emphasis on the situatedness of all writing acts (see *Writing/Disciplinarity*), defines "situation" more broadly, arguing that writing ability can extend and be taught overtly across contexts, at least to a certain extent. Some writers, she argues, can apply some general writing strategies to local rhetorical situations and contexts. If this is not the case, then writers are dependent on an apprenticeship model, which presumes that learning can occur only as a result of immersion in a particular discipline. Soliday argues that, if we believe that the only way that students can acquire new genres is for them to pick them up on their own, without instruction, we may be blocking their access to disciplinary genres.

Soliday uses several research strategies to reach her conclusions, including surveys, interviews, and reflective pieces written by both students and faculty. Citing Lave and Wenger's book *Situated Learning*, she stresses the importance of an "apprenticeship model" (Soliday 6), of linking a genre to social context, and of helping faculty gain awareness of the rhetorical expectations that inform genre within a particular discipline. The book insightfully applies genre theory to disciplinary practice, urging us "to believe that we can find a 'clear path' to genres rather than just 'hoping' students will be able to find a clear path through trial and error" (105). Soliday's study, happily, constitutes a validation of this optimistic perspective.

The concept of genre that informs Soliday's book has been a consistent presence in my classroom teaching, as well as in my scholarly work. I have incorporated it into undergraduate courses, both at the lower and upper division levels, as well as into my graduate seminars. Graduate students are particularly grateful for the insight that genre analysis enables, not only in helping them with their teaching, but also with their own graduate work in seminars and ultimately, in writing theses. Almost twenty years ago, I found the concept of genre to be helpful for my Dutch students, and I expect that Soliday's book will demonstrate the value of genre awareness in a variety of WAC contexts.

Northridge, CA

Works Cited

Devitt, Amy. "Generalizing About Genre: New Conceptions of an Old Concept." *CCC* 44.4 (1993): 573-86. Print.
Graff, Gerald. *Clueless in Academe: How Schooling Obscures the Life of the Mind.* New Haven: Yale UP, 2003. Print
Lave, Jean, and Etienne Wenger. *Situated Learning: Legitimate Peripheral Participation*. Cambridge: Cambridge UP, 1991. Print.
Petraglia, Joesph, ed. *Reconceiving Writing, Rethinking Writing Instruction*. Mahwah: Lawrence Erlbaum, 1995. Print.
Prior, Paul. *Writing/Disciplinarity: A Sociohistoric Account of Literate Activity in the Academy*. Mahwah: Erlbaum, 1998. Print.
Russell, David. "Rethinking Genre in School and Society: An Activity Theory Analysis." *Written Communication* 14 (1997): 504–54. Print.
Swales, John. *Genre Analysis*. Cambridge: Cambridge UP, 1990. Print.
Thaiss, Chris, and Terry Myers Zawacki. *Engaged Writers, Dynamic Disciplines*. Portsmouth: Boynton/Cook Heinemann, 2006. Print
Wardle, Elizabeth. "'Mutt Genres' and the Goal of FYC: Can We Help Students Write the Genres of the University?" *CCC* 60.4 (2009): 765-89. Print.

The Changing of Knowledge in Composition: Contemporary Perspectives, edited by Lance Massey and Richard C. Gebhardt. Logan: Utah State UP, 2011. 335 pp.

Reviewed by Adam M. Pacton, University of Wisconsin-Milwaukee

The Changing of Knowledge in Composition (*CKC*) is a book about a book—*The Making of Knowledge in Composition* (*MKC*)—but it's also a book about a field (or is it a discipline?). It's a book about anxieties and ambivalences, pluralism and cohesion, nihilism and faith. It's a book about composition, and it's a book about Composition.

Nearly a quarter of a century has passed since Stephen North originally published *MKC*, and the questions it raises remain as relevant today as they were in 1987. Is Composition a discipline? Is there a Theory of Composition, or are there only theories? How do we make knowledge in the field, and how can we demonstrate to those outside of the field that what we make *is* knowledge? What methods do we use in our inquiries, and how do we employ them? Is the best that we can build a rambling "House of Lore?"

In many cases, the authors of this collection grapple with the same issues that North did in *MKC*, but to call this volume a mere response would be an egregious misnomer; *CKC* is a reflection. In a number of cases, it is a reflection on *MKC* and how individuals and the field received it. It's also a reflection on some of the most salient problems in Composition today. Perhaps most interesting, however, is the fact that *CKC* is a reflection *of* the field. As the subtitle of *CKC* states, it is a collection of "Contemporary Perspectives," rather than a singular "Portrait of an Emerging Field"; it is not a quasi-ethnographic painting, but instead it is a photomosaic.

Lance Massey and Richard Gebhardt group the essays in *CKC* into four often-overlapping sections. Part 1, Personal Responses to *The Making of Knowledge in Composition*, juxtaposes two personal responses to North's original book: Edward White's "The Significance of North's *The Making of Knowledge in Composition*" and Lynn Bloom's "The World According to North—and Beyond: The Changing Geography of Composition Studies." These two essays capture just how divisive *MKC* was when it was published and how tempers still flare over the book. White fondly remembers North as a firebrand, pointing out foibles and pedantry as he found them, and he believes *MKC* can produce a necessary demythologizing effect for graduate students. Bloom, on the other hand, sees this same fieriness as leading to "scorched-earth scholarship" (33) and laments the time she spent teaching *MKC*.

In part 2, Working the Field: Knowledge-Making Communities Since *The Making of Knowledge in Composition*, the contributors directly engage with a number of central concerns that *MKC* raises. Richard Fulkerson, in "The

Epistemic Paradoxes of 'Lore': From *The Making of Knowledge in Composition* to the Present (Almost)," wonders whether compositionists can find a way to distinguish good lore from bad lore, or whether these efforts are methodologically "predoomed" (60). In "Makers of Knowledge in Writing Centers: Practitioners, Scholars, and Researchers at Work," Sarah Ligett, Kerri Jordan, and Steve Price peruse twenty years of writing center scholarship, coding articles according to North's methodological categories. Their findings point to a widening, and potentially troubling, gap between writing center practices and the types of writing center scholarship that are actually disseminated. Kelly Pender's essay, "Philosophies of Invention Twenty Years after *The Making of Knowledge in Composition*," focuses on North's "Philosophers" category, showing how a vibrant community of "Philosophers" has coalesced around the dialectic between neoclassical and postmodern approaches to invention. Erica Frisicaro-Pawlowski's "Making Knowledge, Shaping History: Critical Consciousness and the Historical Impulse in Composition Studies," presents *MKC* as an early model of the type of critical historicizing that subsequently shaped a great deal of Composition scholarship: *MKC* is the first major work in Composition that focuses on an individual's historical and methodological location within a discipline rather than the discipline's location within larger institutional ecologies. Victor Villanueva's chapter, "Rhetoric Racism, and the Remaking of Knowledge-Making in Composition," takes an opposing critical view of *MKC*, ironically noting that although North repeatedly calls for methodological self-awareness, he is blind to "the biases in his gaze" (122) and deaf to the voices of scholars of color. In short, North never speaks of gender or color in *MKC*—Villanueva points out that no persons of color are cited in *MKC* (122)—let alone the relationship of these identity categories with epistemology in Composition or Rhetoric.

Part 3, *The Making of Knowledge in Composition and Education*: Undergraduate, Graduate, and Beyond, gathers more structural or institutional essays together. Dunn argues, in "Practice as Inquiry, Stephen M. North's Teaching and Contemporary Public Policy," that compositionists need to capitalize on the wealth of scholarship done in the field to help their colleagues, their secondary-school counterparts, and the public at large understand and implement the best practices in writing. North, in his addition to the collection, "On the Place of Writing in Higher Education (and Why It Doesn't Include Composition)," takes a much more insular stance. He feels that the "promise of Composition" (203) to transform the writing practices of a group of heterogeneous college freshmen into something stylistically inoffensive to other faculty, has remained, and will remain, unfulfilled. The only viable corrective is a "writing studies" program populated by self-selected students and faculty not responsible for any universal writing requirement. Joyce Kinkead recognizes the importance of closer professional relationships between writing professors and undergraduate compositionists, and in "Undergraduate Researchers as Makers of Knowledge in Composition in the Writing Studies Major," she urges compositionists to engage in greater collaborative research with undergraduate majors, to both teach future colleagues and to learn themselves. Matthew Jackson echoes the importance of the reciprocal relationship between compositionists and their students in "Pedagogy, Lore, and the Making of *Being*," but he moves beyond knowledge construction and argues that an essential point missed by North is that pedagogical interaction is fundamentally instersubjective: teachers and students not only jointly construct knowledge, but they also jointly constitute one another's being (167).

In the final section of *CKC*, Disciplinary Identities, Disciplinary Challenges: Unity, Multiplicity, and Fragmentation, the contributors try to locate Composition within larger disciplinary and discursive spheres. Drawing on the disciplinary criteria North originally used in *MKC*, Kristine Hansen in "Are We There Yet? The Making of a Discipline in Composition," argues that Composition has not achieved disciplinarity, though it has made some progress since North's original mapping of the field. The creation or adoption of more "writing studies" programs, an increase in writing majors, and a movement to produce greater experimental replication all point to the possibility of disciplinarity; however, a dearth of qualified staff, administration, and institutional support continues to vitiate this possibility (258-59). On the other hand, David Smit, in "Stephen North's *The Making of Knowledge in Composition* and the Future of Composition Studies 'Without Paradigm Hope,'" argues that the increasing situatedness of Composition at theoretical, scholarly, and pedagogical levels (i.e., its postmodern status) precludes any possibility of disciplinarity: if compositionists do not share epistemology, methodology, ontology, or teleology, then there is no way to talk about their differences, let alone their similarities (225). Lance Massey, in "The Dis(Order) of Composition: Insights from the Rhetoric and Reception of *The Making of Knowledge in Composition*," paints a more complicated picture of the field and *MKC*, arguing that both oscillate between modernity and postmodernity in potentially generative ways. Massey also tempers the more apocalyptic and all-or-nothing voices in the field, by arguing that Composition has always been a field in crisis and, "rather than dampen the present sense of urgency, this realization simply reminds us that, while we may never *not* be responding to a crisis of one sort or another, one of our jobs is always to try to understand *this* critical moment as clearly as possible" (319). Patricia Web Boyd, in "Making Space in Composition Studies: Discursive Ecologies as Inquiry," and Brad Lucas and Drew Loewe, in "Coordinating Citations and the Cartography of Knowledge: Finding True North in Five Scholarly Journals," try to understand this critical moment—Boyd explores how Ecocomposition might offer the sort of rich methodological pluralism that is integrative rather than disintegrative, while Lucas and Loewe show how bibliometric analysis could uncover ways in which a seemingly fragmented field can cohere over time through the scholarship its members produce.

CKC should be required reading in every graduate program in Composition, as *MKC* once (largely) was. This collection not only focuses on some of the more pressing issues facing compositionists today, but it also contains some of the most influential voices in the field, and a short review like this one cannot capture their sophistication, elegance, and clarity. True, the voices contained in *CKC* speak in different registers and often at cross-purposes, and some might argue that any coherence in the collection is artificial. But the same arguments have been made about Composition, and these arguments miss the point that univocality or consensus is not a precondition of knowledge, nor is it desirable in many contexts. The variety of perspectives, methodologies, and conclusions in this volume give hope for a robustly pluralistic approach to knowledge-making in Composition, an approach that will not tear itself apart.

Milwaukee, WI

Works Cited

North, Stephen M. *The Making of Knowledge in Composition: Portrait of an Emerging Field*. Portsmouth: Boynton Cook, 1987. Print.

Going North Thinking West, by Irvin Peckham. Logan: Utah State UP, 2010. 176 pp.

Reviewed by Chanon Adsanatham, Miami University

Education is perceived to be the door and ladder to prosperity. Learning, it is believed, will open new opportunities and help one advance intellectually and socioeconomically. As writing instructors, we believe in the transformative potentials of our pedagogy. We teach students to be rhetorical authors and audiences of "texts," believing these abilities will help them attain success in college and beyond, and since the social epistemic turn in the early '90s, composition courses also strive to make learners become critical "readers" of culture; we teach them to challenge hegemonic myths in order to bring about positive social change (Berlin 100-101). Cultural criticism, critical thinking, and argumentation are highly regarded in our discipline. Critiquing these valued practices as middle-class *habiti*, Irvin Peckham's *Going North Thinking West* examines how contemporary composition pedagogy marginalizes working class students, castigating their culture and worldviews. It calls for our discipline to develop a more reflexive and inclusive pedagogy for teaching college composition.

Situating composition studies as a middle-class enterprise, the book begins by problematizing the functions of education. Chapter 1 posits that education does not merely impart knowledge, it disciplines working class students to conform to literacy standards and practices deemed acceptable/appropriate by the bourgeoisie, and it initiates them into a culture that privileges and maintains middle class epistemology and values. This presumption frames the book's remaining arguments.

Chapter 2 provides a definition of class: "a system of social relationships within which people act toward each other as if the groups *did* exist ... sorting on the basis of a person's occupation, level of authority, assets, level of education, and social relationships" (26). Through this definition, chapter 3 explores the relationship between class and language, showing how linguistic codes demarcate status and identity and how first-year writing exacerbates this demarcation by norming the middle-class language. Peckham asserts that composition studies accentuates the "logic of the deficit thesis" through which working-class language is depicted as deficient because it detracts from middle-class English, the so-called "language of power" (42). This logic is then used to justify the adherence to bourgeois language and literacy practices, and instructors come to believe that although students have the right to their own language, they best learn the master's discourse. Working-class speech becomes castigated as a result.

Chapter 4 argues that, like middle-class English, critical thinking is not class neutral. It classifies critical thinking into two strands: cognitive and social. The former focuses on reasoning, correctness, and logical validity (*logos*). The latter analyzes social structure and ideology. Peckham acknowledges that both strands are important, but he advocates teaching them with "epistemological humility" in which students are taught to be reflexive and recognize that all perspectives are partial and situated (64). Hence, it is crucial for students to learn to think through multiple lenses and continuously question their knowledge and beliefs.

Chapter 5 critiques argumentation and shows how it conflicts with working-class learners' background in five ways. First, academic argumentation values objectivity, by which Peckham means composing in a distanced tone with reason, rationality, and logic at the fore, and sublimating emotion and desire that might impede that tone. According to Peckham, this norm is problematic for working-class rhetors because they see emotionally distant discourse as pretentious and insincere; they prefer to "write ragged. Their words spew out, an eruption of thought and emotion..." (71). Second, effective argumentation requires writers to see issues from multiple angles, but working-class students have limited opportunities to cultivate this ability. Peckham claims that, contrary to the working-class, upper- and middle-class Americans are exposed to varied social situations and roles through their networking, employment, and travel. These exposures broaden their perspectives and allow them to see from various points of view. Hence, they have an advantage in academic argumentation over working-class writers (73). Third, dialogism is lacking among working-class members. Given their social position, Peckham believes they are not raised/trained to dialogically negotiate back-and-forth on public issues and often are silenced (73-75). Fourth, middle-class children possess greater vocabulary and syntactic skills. They enter the academy with more advanced language ability (78). Lastly, academic writing encourages readers to read against the grain, practices that Peckham purports are not encouraged in the working-class household, where children are taught to remain silent, defer to authority, and reserve their complaints (79-80, 84-85). In sum, this chapter demonstrates that academic argumentation is not disinterested; it favors bourgeois privileges, putting working-class learners at a disadvantage. Peckham is not suggesting that we cease teaching argumentation, however. Through his critiques, he is attempting to expose the biases of academic conventions so we can better understand and accommodate working-class learners and most importantly, recognize that they may have difficulties acquiring academic conventions because of *habiti* differences—not unintelligence or sloth.

Chapter 6 critiques critical pedagogy. Peckham believes that it focuses on politics at the expense of composing. Ideology, rather than writing, becomes the main subject of the course. Further, critical pedagogues may also position themselves as the enlightened ones and students as the blinded ones, hereby producing a hierarchy that runs counter to the egalitarian aim of critical pedagogy. Moreover, the instructor's urge to correct students' naïve perceptions can lead to a vanguardist pedagogy that pressures students to agree with his/her worldviews. Class discussions become prescribed to assure a predictable agreement, and free, radical thinking is circumvented as a result.

Extending the critique of critical pedagogy, chapter 7 explores how cultural studies lessons can clash with working-class students' *habiti* and, at times, beliefs. An analysis of a textbook and writing prompt on cultural criticism in this chapter shows that they are written in a patronizing tone that positions students as naïve subjects. Peckham also examines a sample student essay on a cultural critique assignment and found that the prompt conflicts with working-class students' beliefs, causing one student to become ambivalent about the course's focus and function. She ended up producing a weak essay for which she received a poor grade. The instructor thought this writer failed to demonstrate the social strand of critical thinking, when in fact, Peckham argues, she is attempting to negotiate and resist the political agenda and middle-class values upon which the course is based (133, 142). According to Peckham, what is at issue here is the clash between middle- and working-class worldviews, but the teacher's bourgeois root and political views may have precluded her from recognizing this (142).

Citing two case studies, chapter 8 demonstrates how critical pedagogues' political orientation may impede them from properly evaluating students' writing. They assess the writer's belief systems instead of his/her prose. Consequently, students may feel pressured to change their viewpoints to align with the instructor in order to please him/her and attain a good grade.

Chapter 9, the last chapter, calls for instructors to practice a reflexive pedagogy that honors and works with, instead of against, working-class students. This does not mean eliminating argumentation or critical thinking. Peckham affirms that these skills are crucial, but in teaching them, we must better understand working class writers and their backgrounds and use this knowledge to create lessons that will engage, rather than alienate, them.

In sum, *Going North Thinking West* urges writing instructors to be critically aware of bourgeois biases inherent in the discipline, so that we can avoid marginalizing writers who may not share that social origin. It invites us to scrutinize our instruction and field at large to create an inclusionary pedagogy for teaching writing. Its critiques of problematic critical pedagogy practices are thought-provoking and significant. They can help us avoid replicating them in our own teaching and maintain a writing-centered classroom that fosters free thinking, open debate, and multivocality, essential for intellectual growth. Altogether, the book aims to break down the steep steps that hinder working-class students from succeeding rhetorically and academically. However, it does not offer concrete pedagogical activities or strategies that might help us circumvent the pitfalls critiqued in the book. How might we foster both strands of critical thinking, maintain epistemological humility, and avoid marginalizing working-class students at the same time? As a composition instructor who works with working-class students, I would have appreciated specific exercises and assignments that would help me address this question in details. Further, while I admire the book's aim, I would like more evidence to substantiate some of the characterizations about working-class learners (e.g. they are less likely to see multiple perspectives).

Regardless, Peckham's book presents a compelling critique of Composition Studies. It encourages us to sustain healthy skepticism by being critical and reflexive about our own teaching and discipline, crucial practices that will help us remain effective and innovative teachers and researchers of writing in the years to come.

Oxford, OH

Works Cited

Berlin, James. *Rhetorics, Poetics, and Cultures: Refiguring College English Studies.* West Lafayette: Parlor P, 2003. Print.

Gramsci and Educational Thought, edited by Peter Mayo. West Sussex: Wiley-Blackwell, 2010. 154 pp.

Reviewed by Kristin Mock, University of Arizona

While Antonio Gramsci has long been an iconic voice in rhetoric and Composition Studies, this international collection of essays, compiled by Peter Mayo at the University of Malta, aims to reintroduce Gramsci's educational thought and practice into twenty-first century Western academic landscapes. With contributors spanning the Americas, Europe, and the South Pacific, the international scope of these essays is impressive, stimulating innovative applications, ideas, and theories for the contemporary classroom and theorist. Strategically adding to the repertoire of writings about Gramsci and emancipatory education, Mayo's collection brings such contemporary topics as global English, feminism, adult education, social work, and modern educational philosophy into active dialogue with Gramsci's writings on hegemony, pedagogy, and social practice. Because of the diversity of topics included, Mayo offers a space for a "rich compendium of writing on Gramsci's relevance to education thought" and a place for scholars to revisit the pedagogic implications of this influential philosopher (3). Educational theory and notions of hegemonic practice—ideas central to Gramsci's work—create the overarching framework and serve as the connective tissue for the eight pieces of scholarship included in this collection.

In the first chapter, "A Brief Commentary on the Hegelian-Marxist Origins of Gramsci's 'Philosophy of Praxis,'" Deb J. Hill challenges enduring notions of education as a liberating force for the masses and asserts that education should allow students to become agents of transformative social change. By calling on Hegel's historical-social view of the subject—in which power is dialectically constituted—and Marx's later theory that the "self" is comprised of various social components (including education), Hill claims that "Gramsci's relentless advocacy for self-education was simultaneously an urging to free minds from the existing capitalist mode of thought" and should continue to dislodge students from their own tendencies to fetishize themselves (6). Hill's piece, which may pose difficulties for those unfamiliar with Gramsci's work, does an excellent job setting up the context for a wider discussion of Gramsci's influence of various disciplines and also provides an extensive bibliography.

Mayo continues the conversation in the following chapter with a more expanded discussion on the relevance of Gramsci's social theories. His contribution, "Antonio Gramsci and his Relevance to the Education of Adults," focuses on the ways in which Gramsci added to Marx's 'base-superstructure' metaphor by examining the contested notion that education is intricately tied to the alteration of class consciousness and social awareness. In terms of pedagogy, Mayo revisits the Italian Factory Council Movement's ideologies and makes the connection that "different sites of social practice can be transformed into sites of adult learning" and that the "subaltern classes" must understand the contextual political nature of their labor situations and be able to critically analyze them from a more distanced perspective (26). Additionally, Mayo explores Gramsci's influence in the areas of pedagogy and language-learning, reminding readers that Gramsci was concerned with "mitigating hierarchical relations between those who 'educate' and 'direct' and those who learn," mastering the dominant language to avoid being relegated to the periphery of political life, and pursuing "multi-ethnic solidarity in an age of globalization" (29, 34). In terms of composition studies, Mayo's essay brings to light the contemporary struggle that adult education and literacy programs face in promoting counter-hegemonic action and is extremely relevant to community literacy practitioners.

Chapters 3 and 4, by John D. Holst and Thomas Clayton, establish a foundation for reading Gramsci's work in modern contexts. Holst's article, "The Revolutionary Party in Gramsci's Pre-Prison Educational and Political Theory and Practice," discusses Gramsci's membership in the Italian Socialist Party, his imprisonment, and the role of education within the revolutionary party. Toward the end of the chapter, Holst develops Gramsci's pre-prison theory in terms of modern practice, claiming that as scholars and teachers we continue working toward a "dialogical, pedagogical, and directive way with the real needs of those most negatively impacted by unfolding socio-political changes" (54-55). Similarly, Clayton, in his piece "Introducing Giovanni Gentile, the 'Philosopher of Fascism,'" brings Gentile's contributions, along with Gramsci's, to the forefront of modern educational debate. Because Gentile, Mussolini's first Minister of Public Instruction, remains a contested political figure, Clayton's piece reminds scholars to always place historical figures within context to avoid misusing or misappropriating them.

Peter Ives revisits Mayo's emphasis on adult education in chapter 5, "Global English, Hegemony, and Education: Lessons from Gramsci," and discusses the contemporary politics surrounding the threat of "global English" on other communities and language groups. Framing the debate around Gramsci's approach to language education, Ives claims that English as "an impediment to counter-hegemonic struggle" is untrue, especially in terms of Gramsci's acknowledgment that learning a dominant culture's language can be liberating for the subaltern classes (94). While Gramsci did promote the argument that the State should dictate language planning for its masses, Ives warns readers to remember that much of Gramsci's writings were in opposition to the Fascist Education Act of 1923, and his work must be analyzed accordingly (85). In arguing that language imposition can and does both liberate and marginalize, Ives effectively problematizes the ideological foundations for implementing a national language on non-dominant groups, and his theory holds true for teachers of language both inside and outside the academy.

In chapter 6, Margaret Ledwith turns the focus to feminism, interrogating the ways in which Gramsci's teachings can be—and are—applied to feminist pedagogy and teaching. Starting with a narrative about her own experience witnessing social inequalities in the classroom, Ledwith provides an excellent gateway for discussing and addressing these issues in practical, pedagogical ways. She suggests, for example, that Gramsci's "insightful analysis of *hegemony*, and the subtle nature of *consent*, offered feminists a conceptual lead on the *personal as political*" and that we can clearly trace Gramsci's influence to feminism's emphasis on cultural identity and difference (101). By tracing the developments of feminist studies over the last forty years, Ledwith skillfully connects Gramsci's teachings with the development of critical consciousness by emphasizing the value of combating powerful hegemonic forces at both the community and academic levels.

Chapter 7, "Towards a Political Theory of Social Work and Education" by Uwe Hirschfeld, explores and redefines the role of social workers and the politicization of their work within the confines of Gramsci's hegemony theory. As Hirschfeld states, there is clearly a potential for social work to become "a critical radically democratic social practice," and yet, many workers in the field have not accepted their role as being equal to those with whom they work, subconsciously creating a superiority complex (114). To transform the industry, he claims, the field must reorient its ideological assumptions; namely, that attempting to "normalize" and "assimilate" seemingly disenfranchised groups is, in fact, securing their marginalization in "mainstream" society and refusing them entrance into the labor market (117). In order for social work to become the foundation for socio-political action, Hirschfeld concludes that social workers must ponder both their personal role and the place of transformative education in their practice, adopt a critical pedagogical stance in their cases, and ensure that their agencies are clean, organized spaces that do not scream "impoverished" but rather promote well-being and security (119).

Concluding the collection, Rosemary Dore Soares' essay, "Gramscian Thought and Brazilian Education," provides a nice complement to Hirschfeld's work, looking at the possibilities for socialist projects in Brazil's public education system and the implications for educational reform in terms of how various Brazilian scholars have read and appropriated Gramsci's work. Though Brazil's education system has been nothing less than tumultuous since the 1920s, Soares does an excellent job historicizing the country's political reforms in terms of education and providing a context for which to read the current debate. By exploring Gramsci's interest in the Communists' concept of the "unitary school," an institution that combines intellectual and industrial work, Soares shows how Gramsci brought renewed interest in public education beginning in the 1980s (140). Today, as Brazil continues to propose new educational models, Gramsci's ideas clearly remain relevant and indispensable.

While this collection is certainly useful for those already engaged in transformative education, scholars in education, rhetoric and composition, English studies, international policy, and social work would find this work particularly insightful to their practice. While clearly targeted to those involved in researching cross-cultural educational thought and practice, it is indeed accessible to a wide range of disciplines and would perhaps be an excellent theoretical resource, in addition to texts that are mostly concerned with classroom dynamics. Instructors and professors in rhetoric and composition who are concerned with the politics of language in the classroom and the difficulties posed by requiring Standard Written English will also find this collection useful for theorizing their teaching practice and understanding diversity in their classrooms. Additionally, researchers, scholars, and teachers interested in promoting social justice and engaging in critical pedagogical practice would also find these applications to Gramsci's seminal text both relevant and timely, especially in regards to understanding the complex relationship between language, education, and policy in contested political spaces.

Tucson, AZ

Writing Against the Curriculum: Anti-Disciplinarity in the Writing and Cultural Studies Classroom, edited by Randi Gray Kristensen and Ryan M. Claycomb. Lanham: Lexington Books, 2010. 235 pp.

Reviewed by Kenny Walker, University of Arizona

Writing Against the Curriculum presents a collection of essays about anti-disciplinary practice within writing programs structured around WID philosophies. In their introduction, the editors contend that this popular restructuring—normally a single first-year "Introduction to Writing" course, followed by a two-year sequence of "Writing in the Disciplines" courses taught in academic departments—essentially reduces first-year composition to a pre-disciplinary course of minor significance and status. But this status also creates a space to infuse FYC with anti-disciplinary praxis. The editors argue that these courses "make excellent spaces to question disciplinarity through the study of rhetoric, the attention to invention and intervention, the emphasis on critical thinking, and […] curricular flexibility […], before students experience disciplinary enforcement most intensely in the advanced classes" (3). In a curricular structure where writing is a gateway for the disciplinary assembly-line, this collection demonstrates the ways in which pedagogies can slow and subvert this process. Audiences of critical pedagogues, writing program administrators, and WAC/WID practitioners who seek a critical approach will find this collection of particular value.

The driving question of the book asks: how can theory and pedagogy work to examine, analyze, and subvert the mechanisms of disciplinarity? A primary answer is to deliberately integrate Composition Studies and Cultural Studies for anti-disciplinary projects, and nearly all eleven chapters in this short collection demonstrate this integration. The book is divided into three sections. The first, "What Is Writing For?", is a meditation on the pedagogical praxis of anti-disciplinarity; the second, "Shifting Schemas," is a critique of curricular and institutional structures, and a demonstration of anti-disciplinary practice in full courses and writing programs; the third, "Writing Across the (Anti) Disciplines," details forms of intervention in disciplinary classrooms, and shows how anti-disciplinary pedagogy opens up new spaces for student agency. One of the strengths of the book as a whole is how it playfully (re)assembles the concept of discipline, both in the Foucaultian sense of restriction, surveillance, and punishment, and in its denotations of methodology, body of knowledge, and a community with shared values. The introduction does a thorough threading of popular prefixes for disciplinary—pre-, inter-, trans-, multi-, anti-, cross-, and post- —and it clearly situates "writing pedagogy as a critical practice against discipline, and towards post-disciplinary," defined here as a pedagogy that functions as if discrete disciplines no longer matter (5). This frames the book as a collection of pedagogies against the dominant methods, knowledge practices, and values of WID structured writing programs. It asserts critical inquiry as a tactical practice to resist these forces.

Part 1 consists of three chapters about anti-disciplinary writing practices. The opening chapter by Ryan Claycomb and Rachel Riedner, "Toward an Anti-Disciplinary Nexus: Cultural Studies, Rhetoric Studies, and Composition," argues that a civic-minded Rhetorical Studies, an activist-oriented Cultural Studies, and a praxis-laden Composition Studies share a common interest in action and empowerment. This, they argue, can form the basis of anti-disciplinary pedagogy (25). A good example of this at the end of part 1 is Pegeen Reichert Powell's essay "Interventions at the Intersections: An Analysis of Public Writing and Student Writing." She analyzes two examples of student-produced public writing and concludes that the divisions between public and academic or disciplinary and anti-disciplinary are unstable, and in practice risk being distinctions without a difference (69). Her examples of student-produced public writing actively challenge academic taxonomies and sanctified modes of knowledge production, arriving at spaces of productive ambiguity where disciplinarity is no longer the point. Powell's example is typical of this section as a whole. Within the structure of a program that unapologetically seeks to produce workers in service of a totalizing market economy, the student writing valued in this collection is political, self-reflexive, public, and laced with critical awareness (13).

Although the book is framed as primarily concerned with the first-year composition course, by part 2 it becomes clear the book is also about praxis in writing program administration, the library, and WID courses. The particular strength of the essays in part 2 is how mindfully they dwell on the boundaries of pragmatism and critical theory. In his discussion of a WID course, Alan Ramón Clinton demonstrates how writing is so manifold in its possibilities, that in addition to writing to learn a discipline, "writing itself is against discipline" (75). His pedagogy frames writing as a technology of invention which can be used as a means of gaining knowledge, as well as thinking against disciplinary boundaries. Similarly, Catherine Gouge's piece on building and administering Web-Intensive Writing Programs acknowledges the troubling implications of online writing classes, but uses their location to cultivate a critical administrative approach for anti-disciplinary interventions. Specifically, this means resisting demands from upper-level administration for the matriculation of high numbers of traditional students by designing these courses solely for adult populations and building critical reflection into the curriculum. Gouge's pithy summary exemplifies just this kind of boundary work between pragmatism and critical praxis inside and outside the program:

> Inside of the program, I have designed courses which offer students a professional certificate that is authorized by a state university in exchange for becoming more critical and aware students and citizens; outside of the

program, I use my role on university college committees as an opportunity to challenge the disciplinary boundaries which seek to reproduce uncritical laborers and consumers. (121)

In his essay in section 2, "The Brake of Reflection: Slowing Social Process in the Critical WID Classroom," David Kellogg acknowledges the overwhelmingly pragmatic ambitions toward vocation that most of our students have and also makes use of reflexive practice. Kellogg uses reflection and reflexivity to slow the process of disciplinarity and create the space for explicit awareness and critique. Kellogg argues that one way to give support to critical reflection in the WID classroom is to "keep WID programs in an English or rhetoric program where such perspectives have a chance to be acknowledged" (107).

The third and last section of the book consists of three chapters which enact anti-disciplinary pedagogy from within the cultural studies-infused composition and literature classrooms. Unfortunately, the last section leaves the connections to anti-disciplinarity vague. This is particularly strange, given that the last two chapters were written by the editors. I was left wondering why the connection between the anti-disciplinary theory in their introduction and the practice in these pedagogical chapters was not made explicit, as they were in the rest of the book. While Eric Lorentzen's essay on teaching Dickens is an exception, anti-disciplinarity nearly disappears in the last section in favor of descriptions of Cultural Studies pedagogies. While the last two essays are dynamic approaches to Black Studies and Performance Studies in the composition classroom, the lack of specific connection to anti-disciplinary practice leaves the end of the book somewhat disjointed. I can only reason that part of this disconnect is due to the fact that these chapters were originally written a number of years ago as journal articles.

Given the recent calls to strengthen the disciplinary status of composition by teaching the content of our discipline, *Writing Against the Curriculum* provides a counter-statement and asks, what benefits can we derive from a continued, but perhaps more deliberate, non-disciplinary status? While this question may accept a low status for composition in the academic hierarchy, it also offers tactical practices to subvert the centrifugal forces of disciplinary power structures. Its aim is to let composition live outside of a disciplined space, to allow for the vagaries of writing instruction, as long as they provide space for students to cultivate their creative and critical capacities. The collection is the first of its kind and it probably won't be the last. With the rising popularity of WID structured writing programs, *Writing Against the Curriculum* provides a timely and needed response for how Composition Studies and Cultural Studies can resist these trends, implement theory across pedagogical and programmatic contexts, and build anti-disciplinary praxis into an increasingly disciplined academy.

Tucson, AZ

Cross-Language Relations in Composition, edited by Bruce Horner, Min-Zhan Lu, and Paul Kei Matsuda. Carbondale: Southern Illinois UP, 2010. 262 pp.

Reviewed by Amanda Athon, Bowling Green State University

Recently, I participated in a conference workshop on issues in teaching English to Speakers of Other Languages. One of the attendees remarked that, because she taught Advanced Writing, she had no need to think about second-language writers. This notion, that second-language writers are easy to identify and do not exist outside of segregated sections of ESOL courses, stems from what the authors of this collection refer to as composition's tacit policy of English Only (1). The policy, which champions standard, academic English above all others, keeps instructors from following the best pedagogical practices for second-language writers. The lack of scholarship and teacher training in language diversity doesn't help, with scholars having a tendency to align themselves on one side of the conversation—either TESOL instructors focusing on ESOL issues or composition instructors focusing on dialects. Given these concerns, Bruce Horner, Min-Zhan Lu, and Paul Kei Matsuda's collection is an important contribution to the field. Issues in language diversity are rarely given attention in the first-year composition classroom, but these essays reveal the benefits of this topic to all composition classes.

The collection features eighteen essays, divided equally between two sections. The first, "Struggling with 'English Only' in Composition," discusses the evolution of language and provides background on how English Only policies have manifested in the college composition classroom. Part 1 has essays from scholars such as John Trimbur, Gail E. Hawisher, Cynthia L. Selfe, and Paul Kei Matsuda. The second section, "Responses to Struggling with 'English Only' in Composition" offers calls to action for increasing linguistic diversity and a discussion of the real challenges presented by attending to these issues. This section begins with Shirley Wilson Logan's discussion of language and ownership and ends with a reflection by Victor Villanueva. Throughout the collection, the authors continually prove the need for language awareness in the classroom. The problem, Horner asserts in the book's introduction, is that instructors falsely assume that their students are native speakers of English (1). By exposing attitudes promoting monolingualism, the book makes clear the need to study, teach, and assess language in all of its variations.

In the first essay of the collection, "Linguistic Memory and the Uneasy Settlement of U.S. English," Trimbur notes the United States' tendency to forget its heritage as a linguistically diverse nation. He provides a historical overview of the evolution of language in the US, including dialects, pidgins, and creoles born out of the travel and expansion of settlers. For example, African American slaves used a type of plantation creole as a form of secrecy, while this creole was sometimes learned by white slave owners to help control slaves (30). Although the nation's forefathers are often heralded for not making English the official language of the colonies, Trimbur references Benjamin Franklin's warning on the increasing numbers of Germans in Pennsylvania, whom he dubs a "colony of aliens" (34). In this way, Franklin bound language to national identity, even class, something that permeates our culture still. Forgetting our history of language, or linguistic memory, leads to the notion that dialects are somehow inferior to standard English.

While Trimbur details our national history of language, Gail Hawisher, Cynthia L. Selfe, Yi-Huey Guo, and Lu Liu discuss the relevance of our individual literacy histories in their essay "Globalization, *Guanxi*, and Agency: Designing and Redesigning the Literacies of Cyberpsace." Their research reveals that our attitudes toward language largely depend on the social ties we make in our communities and families (57). The authors analyze the literacy narratives of two graduate students, Liu and Guo, to study how language learners can form identities and make connections through the internet. Just as community ties can influence our digital literacies, they also shape how and why we learn English. By studying our individual history with language, we can better understand our present attitudes.

A recurrent theme throughout the collection is the importance of teacher training in language diversity. In "The Myth of Linguistic Homogeneity in U.S. College Composition," Matsuda argues that, despite the pressing need, few graduate composition programs offer coursework on issues in ESOL or language diversity. Writing programs assume that students are native speakers of English despite the increasing presence of non-native speakers. The "good writing" we want students to produce is that which shows no features of second language writing. Similarly, in her essay "Living English Work," Min-Zhan Lu describes the extremes that some go to speak English mimicking that of a native speaker, noting an example of South Korean children who undergo surgery to remove bits of their tongues (42). Instead of trying to speak "perfect" standardized English, Lu argues, users of English should embrace its ability to change as a living language, noting that "our sense of ease with a particular usage might inadvertently sponsor systems and relations of injustice" (48). By showing our students models of English that deviate from standard, academic English, we can increase awareness of the changing nature of English. Later in the collection, in "Discourse Tensions, Englishes, and the Composition Classroom," Shondel J. Nero agrees with Lu and reflects on why our culture insists on the existence of language purity. Nero believes that in order to dispel these myths, instructors need to give examples of authors writing in a vernacular, citing Sapphire and Mark Twain as two possibilities.

Elaine Richardson builds on Nero and Trimbur's discussion of language heritage in the US in her essay "'English Only,' African American Contributions to Standardized Communication Structures, and the Potential for Social Transformation." She points out how, historically, few have acknowledged

African Americans' contributions to language and that words such as tote, banjo, juke, and yam have origins in African languages as well as terminology taken from today's hip hop (99). Academic institutions of all levels provide little instruction on the history and influence of African American English, in comparison to the influence of Greek and Latin.

Part 2 of the collection begins with Shirley Wilson Logan's "Ownership of Language and the Teaching of Writing." Logan asserts that greater TA training is needed in language diversity, echoing Matsuda's call earlier in the collection. Most students neither realize that they speak a dialect of English, nor recognize the multiple variations of English. Logan suggests that those who train graduate students for teaching first-year composition ask students to collect examples of vernacular writing that they encounter in a given week, as a method of opening up the conversation about what it means to speak standard English (187-188). By not providing this training in language diversity, we perpetuate a culture of monolingualism.

Further showing the US's attitude of monolingualism in "Why Don't We Speak with an Accent? Practicing Interdepence-in-Difference," Lu Ming Mao cites a $500 fine that a trucker with a heavy accent received from an Alabama police officer. Even though the driver spoke English, the officer felt the driver violated the federal requirement that those possessing a CDL speak enough English to communicate with a police officer (189). Examples like this, Mao claims, show our negative attitudes toward non-standard English (190). If one has an accent, he or she is assumed to be an inferior speaker of English. Much like the other authors in the book, Lu feels a critical change is needed in the way we teach composition to combat these issues of monolingualism. These changes, as Susan K. Miller-Cochran points out in "Language Diversity and the Responsibility of the WPA," must not only happen in the classroom but also program-wide. Miller-Cochran provides five rules that writing program administrators need to follow to accommodate second-language writers (213-215). She dispels the myth that second-language writers all have the same needs, and that these needs are purely grammatical (215). Instead, WPAs should work to train their staff in issues in teaching ESOL and determine reasonable, realistic means of placement.

Throughout the book, the authors are continually in conversation with one another. Many of the authors reference other essays in the collection before they begin their own argument to demonstrate the importance of cross-language conversations. This is undoubtedly a strength of the collection. Still, there are some places, notably part 2, where less summary of prior arguments and more response would have been ideal. Yet, the collection provides excellent insight into the field of language relations, starting conversations that have not been had often enough in Composition Studies. Not only does the collection examine second-language writing issues, but also the broader field of language diversity, instead of treating them as separate, unrelated topics. Scholarship of this nature is often labeled ESOL, as if to say it has no implications for first-year composition, but issues in language diversity are important for those working with native as well as non-native speakers of English. We need reminders that neither we nor our students are native speakers of academic English. *Cross-Language Relations* is an essential read for those who teach composition—regardless of the level or specialization—and is highly recommended.

Bowling Green, OH

Digital Griots: African American Rhetoric in a Multimedia Age, by Adam J. Banks. Carbondale: Southern Illinois UP, 2011. 187 pp.

Reviewed by Jeanne Law Bohannon, Georgia State University

In his first book, *Race, Rhetoric and Technology: Searching for Higher Ground*, Adam Banks evaluates America's technology sector and its perpetuation of racial inequality. Building on some of those themes, he now gives us a backstory of sorts in *Digital Griots: African American Rhetoric in a Multimedia Age*. Banks develops and synthesizes a series of arguments surrounding African Americans' participation in, and resistance to, Western controlling technology narratives. Employing Hip Hop as metaphor and DJs as multi-generational storytellers, he guides readers through a text structured as musical elements, beginning with the *SCRATCH*.

Listeners view a scratch as an interruption, or break, in an otherwise contiguous experience (1). Banks postulates on the implications of such disruptions as purposeful and reflective. On page 2, he articulates his goals: to identify and linger in the scratch between African American rhetoric and multi-media writing, and then to remix both to show how such rhetorical performances can inform our field's movements within new media spaces. The framework of the text hinges on these goals.

In chapter 1, *GROOVE*, Banks argues for connections in digital composition theory and praxis, based on discourses that develop outside of traditional university walls. He situates himself among scholars such as Jackie Jones Royster, Ted Grace, Carmen Kynard, and Jeff Rice, then juxtaposes their works beside scholars from the fields of music history, literature, African American folk tradition, and popular culture. Banks asks and answers two questions: firstly, how can inquiry into African American rhetorical performances develop models of access and authentic technology use; and secondly, how could these new models inform culturally-aware writing instruction to benefit African Americans and their fellow student-scholars in everyday and academic rhetorical growth (14-15).

Banks dubs DJs "digital griots," who draw on generational influences to tell stories in multimodal genres inside and outside of African American discourse communities. The DJ's musical compositions provide key elements that are relevant to academic textual compositions, such as sampling quotes, crate-digging as research, remixing as critical evaluation, and giving shoutouts to credit sources. In multimodal writing, the DJ also uses diverse writing spaces and media to hone his/her storytelling skills. Some of these technologies are culturally well documented (videos, radio, slams), while others are emerging (ITunes, YouTube, Facebook, MySpace). Banks argues that the visuality and orality of these technologies, and their corresponding pedagogical opportunities in multi-modal writing, can be informed by traditional African American rhetorics. *GROOVE* ends as all chapters in this text do, with a shoutout to fellow scholars and rhetorical practitioners, who have worked in the Scratch to create mixes of past and present experiences.

Moving to *MIX* (chapter 2), Banks asserts the DJ's agency and authority in "mixing" together community discourses and rhetorical strategies in writing/telling African American life experiences in the digital age. As a griot, the DJ must employ strategies to not only produce the texts/tracks, but also to connect them seamlessly, with an awareness of audience and style. As he connects the DJ's actions to divergent writing spaces, Banks acknowledges the difficulty inherent in "mixing" the two competing discourses of vernacular/everyday writing and scholarly/academic compositions (51). He further notes the dualistic spaces in which both of these discourses are embedded. First, he describes the tensions that African American scholars must negotiate in how they present community-based compositions to colleagues in academic discourses. Next, Banks challenges scholars to see the value in community discourses as spaces where writing instructors can witness processes of discursive formations. He then moves into a brief overview of his own teaching experiences in tackling such challenges, evaluating the competing communities of writing as he presents a sample of his work with community-based writing courses, complete with reading lists, an abbreviated course design, learning outcomes, and student work from these collaborative endeavors. He links his personal praxis to community rhetorics that resist and contest dominant discourses in composition classrooms. In an honest dialogue with the reader, he owns his subjectivity and advocacy of his community scholarship projects, in which he brought together Syracuse University student-scholars and student-scholars from the surrounding community to create and share writing in diverse media (58-70). In his courses, instructors are not experts who fill students with knowledge, but facilitators and observers of the processes in which students operate. Here again he channels one of the DJ's goals: to mix together tracks into a synchronous composition. In the final pages of this chapter, Banks links his pedagogy to his advocacy of bi-directional informing relationships between community rhetorics and their academic counterparts.

Through *REMIX* (chapter 3), Banks presents digital griots as creative bridge-builders, who link "back in the day" narratives, which Banks defines as stories within African American communities that cause tensions between generations and yet contain a great deal of ethos (87), to future rhetorical exigencies through multi-media discourses. Banks calls out the DJ as a figure who can draw on the ethos of "Old School" rhetorical experiences to forge new African American narratives, thereby synchronizing past and future. In reconciling generational gaps in African American cultural discourses, the DJ maps out new rhetorical paths, and through his performance, encourages ways for young and old generations to speak through what Banks calls a "generational chasm" (103), a communicative disconnect, often exacerbated by technology. For Banks, remixing is a creative act, one that requires griots to cut and paste generational discourses and combine them as tracks into a seamless composition. The DJ also serves as a conduit through which community writers draw on cultural inspiration to re-envision oral, visual, and digital texts. Banks next describes how initiatives such as eBlack Studies serve as important spaces for digital remixes to operate.

Banks connects African American cultural institutions to their digital revisions in *MIXTAPE* (chapter 4). He links his theoretical arguments from previous chapters to practical actions that griots must take in order to reconcile tensions between competing cultural rhetorics in African American communities. Drawing inspiration from Black Theology and Womanist theoretical frameworks, Banks builds a mixtape of African American discourse and rhetorical performances. He reconceptualizes these rhetorics in digital environments and reflects on the tensions inherent in romanticizing African Americans' participation in, and resistance to, technological discourses. For Banks, composition classrooms become practical sites of resistance to Western controlling narratives of homogenization (130). I took this as a call to composition instructors to seek out, in both theory and praxis, vernacular writing practices and weave them into students' rhetorical strategies and authorial agency. Again, in this chapter we see Banks' fierce advocacy for digital access and its innate significance to sharing knowledge. Referencing Black Theology discourse, he then associates access and agency with ethical issues surrounding shared knowledge and collaboration versus solitary writing and plagiarism. He links the theoretical to practical concerns and defines his own pedagogical praxis as he explicates the validity of collaboration in digital spaces (139). He succinctly demonstrates how Compositionists can address two overarching issues for African American student-scholars: firstly, access; and secondly, the role of writing instruction and its complicity in denying cultural and racial diversity on University campuses (137-138). He uses the mixtape as a metaphor for collaboration between past and present rhetorics, as a means to inform future rhetorical performances.

In his concluding chapter, Banks ties together significant elements of his goals then challenges writing instructors to re-think our praxis because of them. He has already affirmed the DJ as a writer and mixer of cultural rhetorics, a legacy of a heritage and the creator of it. He has demonstrated how African Americans have historically informed technologies and how they continue to do so in multi-modal and multi-disciplinary ways. Banks leaves readers with a renewed challenge to view African American rhetorics as remixed conceptions that blend together both community and academic discourses. We should approach African American rhetoric 2.0 as digital humanities discourse, one that informs and is informed by "techno-dialogics" and shared knowledge production. He calls for "bold, creative, innovative use of technologies" (159) and sustained inquiry into the ways African Americans both participate in and resist technology, specifically in regards to access and engaged use. For Banks, the future of composition praxis lies not only in producing multi-modal texts, but also in acknowledging the fact that marginalized rhetorics have informed, and continue to inform, their production.

With its blend of theory and praxis, *Digital Griots* is a good read for composition scholars who want to re-think how we approach community-based rhetorics. It provides a fresh view of how these rhetorics operate in academic spaces. Banks weaves his arguments through both conversational and field-specific language, giving readers a balanced mix of both, and allowing us to share his advocacy and relate it to our own classroom experiences. The book's biggest weakness for me was its lack of pedagogical strategies; I was left wanting a chapter that focused on specific strategies for implementing his teaching models. Regardless, Banks' writing projects and case studies, as well as his call to re-envision African American Rhetoric 2.0, are significant social topics that should inform conversations in our field as it continues to evolve into multi-modalities and multi-disciplinary environments.

Atlanta, GA

The Managerial Unconscious in the History of Composition Studies, by Donna Strickland. Carbondale: Southern Illinois UP, 2011. 147 pp.

Reviewed by Kristine Johnson, Xavier University

Tensions between humanist intellectual values and business logic are clearly visible in American higher education. Directed by economic interests and prevailing business practices, university administrators often aim to make institutions more cost effective by replacing the tenure system—now criticized for being antiquated and inefficient—with large numbers of contingent faculty. Directed by their own economic interests, students may understand their college education as simply a credential they will trade for success in the labor market, and universities have reinforced this understanding by defining students as consumers of their educational product. Composition Studies occupies a difficult position in this increasingly managed educational culture. While the discipline aims to be democratic and inclusive, it is regularly criticized for its complicity in the administrative structures and labor practices that have produced writing programs with tenured faculty administrators—the boss compositionist—and undercompensated, overworked adjunct instructors.

In *The Managerial Unconscious in the History of Composition Studies*, Donna Strickland argues that administration and business logic have always been part of Composition Studies. Yet, teachers and scholars in the field have pushed the managerial into our disciplinary unconscious: they may refuse the managerial and instead produce research on writing theory and pedagogy, or they may frame administrative work as intellectual work that demands specialized knowledge. For Strickland, the growing body of scholarship written by writing program administrators for an audience of writing program administrators is further evidence that management (a term she uses instead of administration) does not occupy a consequential place in Composition Studies. Contending that management is an essential but overlooked factor in both the origin and the development of Composition Studies, she builds a compelling argument for understanding the history of the discipline "as the history of the increasing importance of managers of the teaching of writing" (17). Strickland offers a materialist history of writing programs as workplaces, composition studies as a profession, and teaching writing as an economic activity. The narrative she constructs covers familiar ground, beginning at Harvard in the nineteenth century and ending in the present, but its material focus challenges canonical disciplinary histories and represents a significant contribution to scholarship in composition studies.

Chapter 1 traces how corporate capitalism influenced the emergence of writing programs from writing courses. Strickland outlines the material conditions and cultural values—labor divisions, mechanization, and the feminization of correctness—that shaped early writing programs. In this chapter, the controlling image is a 1907 Edison dictating machine advertisement: a businessman speaks and produces knowledge while a female secretary types and reproduces this knowledge. The early twentieth century introduced a division between conceptual and mechanical labor, and Strickland argues that an analogous division emerged between the mechanical work of English (writing) and the conceptual work of English (literature). Although the split between writing and literature has regularly been associated with an ideological stance that marginalizes writing, she contends that the split was rooted in the desire to make teaching more efficient in the face of more students and more written production. Writing programs were "made possible not by the devaluing of student writing in the university but by its central function in an institution that depended on writing as a tool for surveillance and assessment" (25). Ultimately, these programs became focused on mechanical correctness and staffed largely by white women, which Strickland clearly and persuasively links to the cultural assumption—embodied by the secretary and the schoolmarm—that women are guardians of correctness and virtue.

Strickland forwards a provocative historical narrative of composition studies when she traces how managerial impulses directed the founding of both the Conference on College Composition and Communication in 1949 and the Council of Writing Program Administrators in 1977. Chapter 2 uses the work of George Wykoff to demonstrate that the CCCC was founded to meet the needs of administrators who wanted to control teacher behavior, an argument that challenges the commonplace belief that the CCCC was founded to serve teachers and improve their working conditions. The nascent field of Composition Studies defined its problem not as bad students or unfair working conditions, but as bad teachers who *needed* managing. Strickland illustrates how the CCCC aimed to solve this problem with a research agenda and professionalization—both of which would normalize composition teaching and enable writing program administrators to "extract the proper kind of labor" from teachers (73). The result of this "professionalism in composition studies has tended to enfranchise those involved in the administration of composition more than it has enfranchised the vast majority of teachers of composition" (54). It was the CCCC, she argues, that created the writing program administrator as a subject position and established among its members a strong affective attachment to the rightness of its disciplinary mission: teaching composition.

As the CCCC expanded beyond its original mission, pursing a research agenda and turning away from administrative concerns, the Council of Writing Program Administrators was founded to reclaim this mission. Chapter 3 explores how the WPA attempted to suppress its managerial associations, while providing an intellectual community for administrators. Although Strickland found that the WPA founders were asking intellectual questions about management (particularly questions related to hiring teachers and assessing programs), she notes they attempted to avoid humanistic disapproval of managerial and/or mechanical work. They showed disdain for administrative tasks, reframed writing program administration as scholarly work, and identified themselves, first and foremost, as teachers. In this chapter, Strickland points to two important factors in the development of the WPA—and ultimately Composition Studies. First, she underscores how emotional attachments to teaching function to construct administration as positive work; writing program administrators feel bad and misunderstood, but "they have an essential task: creating a *space* to manage the affect that most everyone else attaches to writing" (90). Second, she describes how members of the WPA actually enjoyed material success in the growing, highly managed multiversity, continuing the normalizing project first initiated by the CCCC (96).

Composition studies has enjoyed material success in part because English departments depend on revenue from writing programs, but Strickland observes that this success coincided with composition scholars promoting narratives of the field's own marginalization and its commitment to radical democracy. Chapter 4 examines how the discourse of democratic pedagogy became normalizing, obscured the managerial, and functioned affectively. She begins the chapter by identifying a slippage in definitions of democracy: composition scholars define democracy as both an ideal (empowering students to create change) and a reality (helping students enter the middle class). In a critical reading of James Berlin, Strickland analyzes this slippage and identifies where Berlin obscures the managerial in his historical writing. She argues that social-epistemic rhetoric became a legitimizing, normalizing discourse in composition studies, which opened space in the discipline for a political agenda (108-110). Berlin perhaps envisioned democratic participation as an end in itself, but Strickland insists both that democracy must mean more than participation in public debate and that our disciplinary allegiance to democratic pedagogy is reinforced—and limited—by emotional, affective perceptions of its rightness (115-118).

Strickland historicizes the managerial in Composition Studies to support a call to action. Against intellectual misgivings about managerial activity, she urges composition studies to embrace management. In the introduction, she argues that members of the discipline should act as critical, managerial intellectuals, which would allow the field to "develop critical interpretations of [writing program management] ... and to generate radical alternatives" (16). In the afterword, she returns to this call to action, offering two implications of embracing the managerial. Concretely, writing program administrators may be open to tweaking, combining "cultural-critical abilities" with administrative work because they are not affectively attached to particular normalizing commitments (120); and theoretically, they may adopt "operative reason," which unlike instrumental reason does not anticipate outcomes but may be a catalyst for change (121). Although these implications are certainly generative, I found that they provided a weak conclusion to a strong book. The conclusions Strickland draws about operative reason and tweaking seem indirectly related to her historical narrative, but I was further dissatisfied with her conclusions because they addressed the work of writing program administration—and primarily an audience of writing program administrators. For the book to fulfill its aim of reaching the discipline of composition studies, Strickland must also provide conclusions that include this broader audience in her call to action.

The Managerial Unconscious offers fresh, important historical perspectives on Composition Studies as a discipline and writing programs as workplaces. Its contribution to the discipline is primarily as historical scholarship, though it will also be useful for readers interested in affect and composition studies. Finally, it is well theorized, joining composition theory with contemporaneous management theories in a way that suggests new perspectives on both areas of inquiry. Throughout the historical narrative, Strickland illustrates how economic interests and business practices have always influenced composition studies and educational institutions—with varying pedagogical and disciplinary outcomes. As our discipline exists in increasingly managed institutions with increasingly complex economic pressures, this book is an essential resource for readers interested in the history or future of composition studies.

Cincinnati, OH

Beyond Postprocess, edited by Sidney I. Dobrin, Jeff A. Rice, and Michael Vastola. Logan: Utah State UP, 2011. 238 pp.

Reviewed by Timothy Oleksiak, University of Minnesota—Twin Cities

In *Beyond Postprocess*, Dobrin, Rice, and Vastola gather a number of powerful voices in the field of writing studies to "rethink postprocess in terms of potentialities for philosophical revisions and the institutional failures thereof" (2). This collection resists presenting a singular stance on what it means to be beyond postprocess. Rather, Dobrin et al. aim to set the stage for a broad reevaluation of writing studies. To do so, they organize the book into three areas. Part 1 offers theoretical interventions into postprocess theory. Part 2 suggests ways in which developing new media technologies require writing studies professionals to move beyond postprocess. Finally, part 3 critiques what could be called the pedagogical imperative animating the majority of writing studies work. Generally speaking, this is a challenging text with ideas that push hard against disciplinary and theoretical assumptions about agency, pedagogy, and what it means to study writing in the twenty-first century. By many accounts, this collection is successful in providing foundations on which further conversations about the study of writing should be built. In this review, I pay particular attention to six of the more provocative arguments throughout the collection. Nevertheless, each essay is thoughtful in its own right and deserves critical attention.

Kent's opening preface offers a useful overview of postprocess theory's basic tenants: principle of charity, hermeneutic guessing, etc. In their introduction, Dobrin et al. distinguish Kent's *Post-Process Theory: Beyond the Writing-Process Paradigm* from their own. Dobrin et al. suggest Kent's version of postprocess theory situates itself in opposition to a standard paradigm of process theory in order to identify the problematics with process theory's animating assumptions (1). *Beyond Postprocess* argues that early theories of postprocess were too oppositionally constructed. This new collection moves beyond that oppositional construct. The result is that the two collections become companion pieces rather than challenges to each other for theoretical supremacy.

Barbara Couture's "Writing and Accountability" begins part 1. For Couture, writing in a postprocess era requires that assessment of writing includes a way to account for the ways that writers engage the other and the other's experience in the development of writing. Couture asserts that to be accountable as a writer, individuals must understand that the other always already sets the conditions through which writers' ideas are formulated. To achieve this understanding, theorists of writing must consider how writing functions, not as an articulation of the self, but as part of the way writers establish and maintain relationships with others (39).

Byron Hawk's "Reassembling Postprocess: Toward a Posthuman Theory of Public Rhetoric" is a standout essay in this section. Hawk's articulation of posthuman is a lucid and nuanced critique of the humanist assumptions animating process and postprocess theories. For Hawk, postprocess creates theoretical concepts that are still bound by social constructionist epistemologies and traditional hermeneutics (75). This centering of human agents has blinded our field to the ways in which humans' embodied relationships are connected with ever-changing non-human objects of varying scales (77). In order to break from the subject-centeredness that characterizes both process and postprocess, writing theory that is beyond postprocess will need to become posthuman.

Part 2 centers on new media's relationship to postprocess theory. Jeff Rice's "Folksonomic Narratives: Writing Detroit" distinguishes folksonomic narrative from Helen Foster's concept of networked subjectivity. Rice contends that folksonomic narratives reject the notion of a singular space and convention (122) that are important to networked subjectivities. Rice illustrates his understanding of folksonomic narratives through a "little narrative" (123) of Detroit. Detroit—as a general object of discourse—carries the tags "ruins," "emptiness," or "decline," (120) yet these tags exist as part of a constellation of tags that also include "Model T," "automobile," and "industrialization" (123). This constellation gives rise to the spaces whereby multiple meanings co-exist in the *same* space and object. Using tags to freely float in a narrative is part of a folksonomic rhetoric that moves beyond a specific rhetorical situation and toward "little narratives" that are neither hierarchic nor invite closure.

In "Old Questions, New Media," Kyle Jensen makes the case for the development of what he calls "online writing archives" (133). Jensen suggests that online writing archives would "consciously expose" (133) variations in writing, as well as provide a space for collaboration between scholars and students of writing. He outlines five basic features of the online writing archive: it must provide every aspect of a work's revision history; it must be intelligible to its users; it must use digital technologies in ways that distinguish the archive from traditional print codexes; it must attend to the material conditions of technology; and finally, it must acknowledge the way technology shapes the reception of the texts located in the archive (136-137). The online archive is a mode of inquiry beyond postprocess, as it allows users to shape and expand the archive. It's dynamic nature, according to Jensen, can yield new insight into how writing works.

I would be remiss if I did not articulate my frustration with an obvious oversight in Jensen's essay. Jensen's work references a figure to help explain the online writing archive; however, the figure does not appear anywhere in the book. Such a mistake is unfortunate, given the significance of the figure in helping Jensen articulate his important contribution to textual archives.

Part 3 critiques classroom/pedagogical imperatives animating writing studies scholarship. In "First, A Word," Raúl Sánchez argues that it is an error to think that process and postprocess theories are substantively and epistemologically distinct (184). For Sánchez, both theories envisioned a subject in control of the writing situation, albeit from different angles. For process, the subject-orientation was toward the writers of texts. By positioning itself too closely as a reaction against process, postprocess theory makes its concern a critique of the subject. Such a critique reifies the subject-orientation. The critique of subject-orientation implies that writing theorists must work on the relationship between culture, pedagogy, and writing to reveal that writing is both culture and pedagogy, neither of which are solely guided by classroom concerns (193).

In "The Salon of 2010," Geoffrey Sirc suggests that the bracketing of imaginative possibilities within postprocess theory necessitates a break with postprocess theory writ large. Because its insistence on theoretical constructs that exist outside the empirical world, "postprocess has restored the strict delimitation between composition and creative writing that was beautifully blurred in the process era" (205). Moreover, postprocess's "fatal gesture" was its willingness to separate itself from the craft of writing by focusing instead on the effects of writing (215). Postprocess theory's failure to account for the pleasures of "modernism's *making*" (216) is precisely what necessitates a return to process. Yet as we return to process, we should carry with us the technological tools of the present in order to "refigure the classroom as a studio where students can create movies, collages, mixtapes, playlists, websites, podcasts, Photoshop parodies" (216). The technological "makings" allow ideas and texts to circulate in ways that move passions and ignite critiques. Writing in the salon of 2010 does work knowing full well that the work it does cannot be understood prior to its making. Moving beyond postprocess is to recall that textual production is still important to communication.

By means of a conclusion, I want to identify what I believe to be a missed opportunity. I see no reason why the conversations that are important to our field must always and exclusively take place within a scholarly press *printed* book or journal. The textbook industry—with its links to websites and companion CD-ROMs—could teach us some valuable lessons on this point. I offer one alternative possibility here. YouTube can function as a scholarly space if only we would make it so. Could not Utah State UP have worked with editors and contributors to develop a YouTube channel that allows those who read the book the opportunity to continue the discussion of these concepts online? What if, in addition to the essays written for this collection, the contributors also prepared 10-minute YouTube videos that extend the discussions that their contributions make?

These questions about *how* writing should be delivered are keeping within the spirit of *Beyond Postprocess*. Such new media or digital spaces might contribute in innovative ways to the development of online writing archives. Attention to how we present knowledge about writing might be a part of the salons of 2010 and beyond. These are questions not directed *against* the book. They are questions asked because the arguments within it encourage such asking. Ultimately, the generative power of *Beyond Postprocess* makes it a collection worthy of careful attention and robust response.

Minneapolis, MN

Works Cited

Kent, Thomas, ed. *Post-Process Theory: Beyond the Writing-Process Paradigm.* Carbondale: Southern Illinois UP, 1999. Print.

Rhetoric's Earthly Realm: Heidegger, Sophistry, and the Gorgian Kairos, by Bernard Alan Miller. Anderson: Parlor P, 2011. 387 pp.

Reviewed by Ira Allen, Indiana University, European Graduate School

It's always a good time for a book about *kairos*, rhetoric's most time-oriented concept. But the present moment, as our shared world reorders itself in particularly drastic ways, is especially fine for Bernard Alan Miller's *Rhetoric's Earthly Realm*. Miller offers, via Gorgias and Heidegger, a worldview that underscores our caught-upness in language and accepts *kairos* as language's transformation of the world *in* and *as us*. Readers will probably agree with Miller that, by contrast, Plato's version of *kairos* scrabbles too desperately for mastery of language, or that other "right-timing" rhetorical readings of *kairos* overemphasize an idea of the rhetor as sovereign subject, swaying audiences with just-in-time delivery. Whether compositionists are prepared to open up to the trickster *kairos* that Miller discerns in Gorgias and Heidegger, however, is an open question.

On the whole, and despite real difficulties on the Heidegger side of things, they should. Miller asks us to accept a vision of the Gorgian *kairos* as marking the moment and mode of our being overcome by language, such that we in turn serve as conduits for language's overcoming of others and itself (316-18). In this, the central insight motivating *Rhetoric's Earthly Realm* is as crucial as ever, and deserving of the deep engagement Miller requests of us: language is both *greater than* and *what* we are. In tracing out what this means for rhetoric, returning always to *kairos* as a rhetorical term of art, Miller takes up a host of other key terms, Greek and otherwise: *physis*, mystery, *xa*, racial memory, *doxa*, *Augenblick*, and *Dasein*, not least of all. In succession, each comes to identify with some or all of the others before finding new definition in opposition to them; along the way, *doxa* re-emerges (not unproblematically) as glory, *physis* presents as the linguistic upsurge of being that allows *Dasein* and Being to be differentially together, and language reigns over and within all as *dynastes*: *logos* as the trickster personification of both word and reason, "the terrible secret of the irrational in the flesh" (243). Even—and perhaps especially—for compositionists wary of rhetorical theory without a clear pedagogical payoff, *Rhetoric's Earthly Realm* is a valuable read.

Those only interested in the concept of *kairos* will be especially well-served by chapters 2 and 3, "The Platonic *Kairos*" and "The Gorgian *Kairos*." These perform important conceptual work in situating *kairos* between philosophical and rhetorical traditions, suggesting that neither has yet come quite to terms with the *kairotic* implications of Gorgias' vision of language as *dynastes*, as a ruler. To really grasp these implications, the unfurling of Miller's entire text is perhaps as important as its conclusions, but the reader pressed for time (or indifferent to Heidegger) might turn directly from chapter 3 to chapter 6 ("Paradox and the Power of the Possible: *Kairos* as the Mark of the Trickster"), the last in *Rhetoric's Earthly Realm*. Where Miller is concerned in early chapters to draw out clearly, in more or less hermeneutic fashion, the thinking of Plato and Gorgias—with the result that the pacing of those chapters, while moderate, is rarely challenging—by the close of the text he has worked himself into something of a frenzy. So many terms are buzzing about, partially identified with and partially disjunct from or even logically antecedent to one another, that chapter 6 seems authentically to have submitted to language's calling. In Heidegger's idiom, which Miller follows throughout, the ek-static frenzy of the text in this final chapter bears witness to the Saying of language. The result is a sense of or feeling for *kairos* as language's appropriation of us, its supposed users. In opening and listening to this appropriation of us by a movement internal to language itself, we partake of a power as much magical as technical, a world-naming and world-changing power that moves us from the everydayness of given situations to the authenticity of new encounters with the linguistic limits of our being.

But what, the practical-minded will ask, does that *mean*? Miller himself is short on examples, though his readings of authors ranging from Heidegger and Paul Tillich, to N. Scott Momaday and his own student Carry Moccasin, are generally compelling. To take a timely instance of the basic point, consider the Occupy movement. Something today has changed, if we view this from the perspective Miller details, within the flows of language (the workings of financial capitalism certainly count as "language" in this capacious conception). It now makes sense to thousands of people, perhaps even millions, to hold strikes without union leadership, to occupy foreclosed homes and businesses, to demand new and revised constitutions; this making-sense is at once deeply linguistic and ineluctably physical—the forces of *doxa* are internally divided, such that *doxa* begets para-*doxa* of its own accord and in thus begetting calls forth new names for Being. "Occupy" is the name for *kairos*' new making-sense, to which we submit more or less poetically, with greater or lesser piety regarding the name itself, but with a certain helplessness vis-a-vis the phenomenon inseparable and even indistinct from that name. More prosaically, in the composition classroom, Miller's trickster *kairos* might be the everyday reordering of selfhood accomplished in students' (and instructors') listening in ever-novel ways to the always-yet-to-be-invented norms of academic writing and thought. Indeed, I can imagine an uptake of *Rhetoric's Earthly Realm* that returns to and reinvigorates both the critical reading and expressive writing sides of the old Bartholomae-Elbow debate.

I mentioned, however, that Miller's text has a Heidegger problem. What are any of us to do with Heidegger's Nazism, now well established as to depth and significance (see, for instance, Rockmore or Faye)? It seems a quiet but broad consensus has emerged to treat Heidegger's Nazism as distinct from his philosophy, and Miller is only too glad of this, devoting two light paragraphs to circumnavigating the matter at the close of the introduction to *Rhetoric's*

Earthly Realm and concluding, "I will speak no more of Heidegger's politics" (33). The opposing view, held by an ever smaller but still vocal minority, may be summed up in a single abrupt statement: "But he was a *Nazi!*" Neither stance is satisfactory, and though I would rather not need to speak here of Heidegger's Nazism, focusing instead only on Miller's very fine—excellent, even—treatise on *kairos*, the strain of Heidegger's philosophical thought most conducive to his Nazism presents a real difficulty for *Rhetoric's Earthly Realm*. Chapters 4 and 5, "*Das Sein*, *Dasein*, and *Doxa*: Attending to the Way of Heidegger's Thought" and "Heidegger and the Gorgian *Kairos*," are thus on the one hand a useful primer to Heidegger's thinking on language, with significant cross-cultural resonance and real payoff for our understanding of Gorgias; on the other hand, however, they also put forward uncritically a Heideggerian nativism that too readily sets the mystery of Being equivalent with language's Saying to and for a given *Volk* or people.

One way to grasp the difficulty here is through Miller's equation, following Heidegger and putatively Gorgias as well, of *doxa* with glory. As Miller has it, *doxa* is at once "the sheer presence of things believed" (55) and "the past as presence ... events instilling reverence and awe from which we draw life in a process sufficiently intense to transfigure particular times and places" (188). As such, it can be read together with the Vietnamese notion of *xa* (the idea of a village as "village" both is and *means* life-world [149-150]) or the idea of "racial memory" as the simultaneous story and reality of Native American history in its undyingness—and Miller is to be commended for his cross-cultural aspirations. On this view, all *doxa* contains within itself the impetus toward its own overcoming, toward para-*doxa*. On the one hand, then, as Being itself structured as the language of a people, a *Volk*, *doxa* is at once the forceful and absolutely physical self-transcendence of *physis*, of Being, and the glory of a particular people's listening to the authentically linguistic character of Being. On the other hand, *doxa* is necessarily also a trickster of sorts, and it is the very moment of its turning on itself that Miller calls *kairos*.

Thus far, well and good, if a little complex. But we must ask—as Miller ought to have done—what makes "a people" plausibly the anchor of language? (Walter Benjamin, for instance, sees the essence and anchor of language not in a *Volk* but in translation itself, in the relation between languages [70-82].) What defines "a people" in this schema? And by what right can *doxa*, even as the materiality of a people's beliefs may provoke an encounter with the event of language as such, be equated with glory when it is equally the case that *doxa* often provokes no awareness at all of language's status as *dynastes*? These are questions Miller does not answer, but we know well the phrase that hangs over Heidegger's responses to all three: *Blut und Boden* (201).

All this points once more to the need, when engaging closely with Heidegger's thought, to attend to the political possibilities carried in that thought. Indeed, Miller might have done just that had his emphasis on listening with Heidegger to Being brought him also to Krista Ratcliffe's excellent *Rhetorical Listening: Identification, Gender, Whiteness*. This particular lack of listening on Miller's part should not, however, stop compositionists and other rhetorical theorists from turning to his wide-ranging text for a deeper and broader understanding of *kairos*. In short, though harboring a troubling political *doxa*, *Rhetoric's Earthly Realm* remains an ambitious, consistently engaging, and useful text, deserving of a wide readership.

Eugene, OR

Works Cited

Benjamin, Walter. *Illuminations*. Trans. Harry Zohn. New York: Schocken Books, 2007. Print.

Faye, Emmanuel. *Heidegger: The Introduction of Nazism into Philosophy in Light of the Unpublished Seminars of 1933-1935*. New Haven: Yale UP, 2009. Print.

Heidegger, Martin. *Being and Truth*. Trans. Gregory Fried and Richard Polt. Bloomington: Indiana UP, 2010. Print.

Ratcliffe, Krista. *Rhetorical Listening: Identification, Gender, Whiteness*. Carbondale: Southern Illinois UP, 2005. Print.

Rockmore, Tom. *On Heidegger's Nazism and Philosophy*. Berkeley: U of California P, 1992. Print.

Contributors

Annette Arrigucci graduated with an MA in Rhetoric and Writing Studies from the University of Texas at El Paso in 2008. She currently works as an online editor for the *El Paso Times*.

Mariaelena Bartesaghi (PhD University of Pennsylvania) is Assistant Professor of Communication at the University of South Florida. Her work examines the process of institutional truth construction, in the relationship between talk and text.

Beth Brunk-Chavez is the Director of First-Year Composition at the University of Texas at El Paso. She also serves as an Associate Dean in the College of Liberal Arts. Her research and publications focus on Writing Program Administration, writing with technology, and teaching with technology.

Ivan Davis is an Assistant Professor of English at Andrews University, where he directs the writing program. His research interests include early twentieth century composition history, particularly assessing the influences on, and the collaborations involving, Fred Newton Scott. His work has appeared in the *Michigan Academician* and *Pedagogy*.

Janet Gebhart Auten directs the Writing Center and teaches the graduate seminar in composition pedagogy for the Department of Literature at American University. She is associate editor of the peer-reviewed journal, *Writing Lab Newsletter* and has published work on teacher response to student writing and writing center pedagogy.

Laurie Grobman is a professor of English and Women's Studies and the coordinator of the Laboratory for Public Scholarship and Democracy at Penn State Berks. She recently published *Undergraduate Research in English Studies* (2010, co-edited with Joyce Kinkead). Grobman's teaching interests center on public scholarship.

Kate Pantelides is a doctoral candidate in Rhetoric and Composition and the Writing Center Coordinator at the University of South Florida. In addition to her decade of work in the Writing Center field, her research interests include Writing Program Administration, composition pedagogy and feminist rhetoric.

Brian Ray is completing his PhD in English at the University of North Carolina at Greensboro. He has also published in the *Journal of Basic Writing* and has written reviews for *JAC*, *Rhetoric Review*, and *TETYC*.

Christian Weisser is an Associate Professor of English at Penn State University, Berks Campus. He currently serves as the coordinator for the BA in Professional Writing and the Writing Across the Curriculum program at Penn State Berks.

MLA's essential standard guide for graduate students, scholars, and professional writers

"The bastion of scholarly publishing etiquette."
—*Bookpage*

"This third edition of the manual is indispensable. ...Essential."
—*Choice*

MLA Style Manual and Guide to Scholarly Publishing, 3RD EDITION

The third edition of the *MLA Style Manual* offers complete, up-to-date guidance on writing scholarly texts, documenting research sources, submitting manuscripts to publishers, and dealing with legal issues surrounding publication.

xxiv & 336 pp.
Cloth ISBN 978-0-87352-297-7
$32.50

LARGE-PRINT EDITION
Paper ISBN 978-0-87352-298-4
$37.50

Join the MLA and receive 20% off the listed price.

"This edition moves MLA's scholarly guidance into the twenty-first century in ways that most of us would never have expected."
—*Writing Lab Newsletter*

Modern Language Association | MLA

Phone orders 646 576-5161 ▪ Fax 646 576-5160 ▪ www.mla.org

THE AUTHORITATIVE GUIDE TO MLA STYLE

Buy access online at www.mlahandbook.org and start using it today.

A print copy will be mailed to you.

Join the MLA and receive 20% off **the listed price.**

Recipient of *Choice* Award for Outstanding Academic Title

Searchable Web site features

- the full text of the *MLA Handbook*
- over two hundred additional examples
- research project narratives, with sample papers

You can also buy the print edition. An access code in the back allows you to use the Web site.

xxii & 292 pp.
Paper 978-1-60329-024-1 $22.00
LARGE-PRINT EDITION
Paper 978-1-60329-025-8 $30.00

Visit the MLA's channel on YouTube at
www.youtube.com/user/ModernLanguageAssoc.

Modern Language Association | **MLA**

Phone orders 646 576-5161 ■ Fax 646 576-5160

An Expert Guide to Current Scholarship

Introduction to Scholarship in Modern Languages and Literatures
3RD EDITION

David G. Nicholls, ed.

The third edition of the MLA's widely used *Introduction to Scholarship in Modern Languages and Literatures* features sixteen essays by leading scholars designed to highlight relations among languages and forms of discourse.

The volume is organized into three sections

"**Understanding Language**" provides a broad overview of the field of linguistics, with special attention to language acquisition and the social life of languages.

"**Forming Texts**" offers tools for understanding how speakers and writers shape language; it examines scholarship in the distinct but interrelated fields of rhetoric, composition, and poetics.

"**Reading Literature and Culture**" covers textual and historical scholarship; interpretation; comparative, cultural, and translation studies; and the interdisciplinary topics of gender, sexuality, race, and migrations (among others).

"*This is a remarkable collection of essays. It brings together some of the best scholars in the field to explore what is involved in the study of languages, texts, and cultures.*"
— Simon E. Gikandi
Princeton University

ix & 371 pp. • 6 x 9
Cloth 978-0-87352-597-8 • $40.00
Paper 978-0-87352-598-5 • $25.00

Modern Language Association **MLA**

Phone orders 646 576-5161 ■ Fax 646 576-5160 ■ www.mla.org

Rhetoric & Writing PhD Program

Preparing Rhetoric and Composition Faculty for 30 Years

Since its founding in 1980, Bowling Green State University's program has prepared more than eighty graduates for faculty careers in rhetoric and composition. Students and faculty in the Rhetoric & Writing PhD Program are committed scholar-teachers who utilize a range of approaches—rhetorical, cultural, empirical, technological—that characterize rhetoric and composition in the twenty-first century.

Some highlights of the Rhetoric & Writing PhD Program:

- Eight core courses in history, theory, computer-mediated writing, research, scholarly publication, and composition studies as a discipline, plus electives in rhetoric and composition and related areas of scholarly interest to students.
- Professional development involving mentoring, collaboration, a monthly colloquium series, and post-prelim groups emphasizing dissertation work and the job search.
- Varied assistantship assignments (FYW, intermediate writing, writing center, faculty research, editorial work, program administration, community outreach, etc.) and competitive non-service fellowships in the fourth year of funding.
- Four-year graduation rate typical for full-time students.
- 100% placement rate among program graduates.

Rhetoric & Writing PhD Program
http://www.bgsu.edu/departments/english/rcweb/index.html
Facebook Group: BGSU Rhetoric & Writing

Program Director, Kristine Blair
kblair@bgsu.edu
English Graduate Office: 419-372-6864

WESTERN STATES RHETORIC AND LITERACY CONFERENCE
Call for Papers

TRANSNATIONAL RHETORICS AND LITERACIES

October 19-20, 2012   University of Winnipeg   Winnipeg, Manitoba, Canada

Keynote Speaker: Diana Brydon, Canada Research Chair in Globalization and Cultural Studies

Transnational rhetorics, broadly defined, are those concerned with broadening knowledge bases beyond the "West," examining discourses, literacies, and Englishes that move beyond our current educational, political, and social systems of the "Global North."

The Western States Rhetoric and Literacy Conference was created to allow scholars in the Western region to come together and exchange current research in rhetoric and literacy studies. While we especially welcome proposals that address the theme for each particular year, we may also consider proposals that deal with other relevant topics and issues. Of particular interest are presentations that encourage audience participation and discussion, and contribute closely to the conference theme and to questions concerning aspects of the following:

- Transnational literacies and cross-cultural learning
- Transnational and diasporic identities
- Resistance, protest, and silence in transnational spaces/movements
- Visual or multimodal rhetorics of transnationalism
- Transnational agency and empowerment
- Transnational institutions, programs, and/or disciplines
- Transnational media and technologies
- Transnational pedagogies
- Practices of representation and transnational circulation
- The politics of translation and/or multilingual writing in and across national borders
- Rhetorics of reconciliation, human rights, and peacemaking in transnational contexts

Please submit your proposals to wsrlc2012@gmail.com (Subject line: WSRL TRANSNATIONALISM PROPOSAL) by May 10, 2012. We ask that you attach

- A proposal (maximum 500 words) in MS Word format or PDF prepared for blind review.
- A 50-word (maximum) abstract that summarizes your conference paper also in MS Word or PDF, accompanied by the title of your paper, author name(s), and affiliation(s).
- An indication of whether you will be giving a **20-minute paper**, which will be combined with others of a similar topic, to form a 90-minute panel OR **a 90-minute panel**, limited to 3 speakers.

Please note that the Western States Rhetoric and Literacy Conference has a NO MULTIPLE SUBMISSIONS policy. Only 1 submission per person.

For more information about the conference, contact, Jennifer Clary-Lemon j.clary-lemon@uwinnipeg.ca

As is our tradition, there is no registration fee for this year's conference.

Graduate Study at Arizona State University
DEPARTMENT OF ENGLISH

MA Rhetoric and Composition
PhD Rhetoric, Composition, and Linguistics

FACULTY

Patricia Boyd | Alice Daer | James Gee | Maureen Daly Goggin (Chair)
Peter Goggin | Mark Hannah | Elisabeth Hayes | Kathleen Lamp | Elenore Long
Paul Kei Matsuda | Keith Miller | Ersula Ore | Shirley Rose | Doris Warriner

The Department of English at ASU has created a diverse and energetic intellectual atmosphere within which to pursue graduate studies. Boasting one of the largest, most productive faculties in the western United States, the department is highly regarded for its professional development and mentoring programs, which prepare students for successful careers in academia and beyond.

english.clas.asu.edu/graduate

DEPARTMENT OF WRITING STUDIES
UNIVERSITY OF MINNESOTA

Study at a research-intensive university with an internationally recognized faculty in one of the longest established rhetoric & scientific and technical communication programs in the country. In addition to our rich history, we have a new commitment to Writing Studies as a field involving research and teaching about global, social, and the digital dimensions of writing.

M.A. and Ph.D. Degrees in Rhetoric and Scientific and Technical Communication
Our program combines theory and research in all aspects of writing, rhetoric, and technical communication. The Ph.D. is in high demand; all of our graduates have placed in academic or industry positions.

M.S. and B.S. Degrees in Scientific and Technical Communication and the Technical Communication Certificate
Designed for working professionals and other students whose primary goal is a career in the field of technical communication.

To find out more visit www.writingstudies.umn.edu

GenAdmin: Theorizing WPA Identities in the 21st Century

Colin Charlton, Jonikka Charlton, Tarez Samra Graban, Kathleen J. Ryan, and Amy Ferdinandt Stolley. 2011.

GenAdmin examines identity formation in a generation of rhetoric and composition professionals who have undergone explicit preparation in scholarly dimensions of writing program administration. The authors argue for "GenAdmin" both as an intellectual identity and as a contingent philosophy of writing program work.

2012 Titles of Interest

Writing Program Administration at Small Liberal Arts Colleges by Jill M. Gladstein and Dara Rossman Regaignon

The Available Means of Persuasion: Mapping a Theory and Pedagogy of Multimodal Public Rhetoric by David M. Sheridan, Jim Ridolfo, and Anthony J. Michel

Writing a Progressive Past: Women Teaching and Writing in the Progressive Era by Lisa Mastrangelo

Locating Visual-Material Rhetorics: The Map, the Mill, and the GPS by Amy D. Propen

On the Blunt Edge: Technology in Composition's History and Pedagogy edited by Shane Borrowman

The Uses of Grammar 2e by Judith Rodby and W. Ross Winterowd

Greek Rhetoric Before Aristotle 2e by Richard Leo Enos

Writing in Knowledge Societies edited by Doreen Starke-Meyerring, Anthony Paré, Natasha Artemeva, Miriam Horne, and Larissa Yousoubova

The entire Parlor Press catalog will be out in ePub, iPad, and Kindle format in 2012!

www.parlorpress.com

www.ingramcontent.com/pod-product-compliance
Lightning Source LLC
Chambersburg PA
CBHW031631160426
43196CB00006B/370